POCKET BATTLESHIPS OF THE
DEUTSCHLAND
CLASS

Admiral Graf Spee after the spring 1938 modifications to the bridge tower.

POCKET BATTLESHIPS OF THE
DEUTSCHLAND
CLASS

Deutschland/Lützow • Admiral Scheer • Admiral Graf Spee

GERHARD KOOP and KLAUS-PETER SCHMOLKE

Naval Institute Press
ANNAPOLIS, MARYLAND

Copyright © Bernard & Graefe Verlag, Bonn, 1990

This edition first published in Great Britain in 2014 by
Seaforth Publishing,
Pen & Sword Books Ltd,
47 Church Street,
Barnsley S70 2AS

Published and distributed in the
United States of America and Canada by the
Naval Institute Press,
291 Wood Road, Annapolis,
Maryland 21402-5034

www.nip.org

Library of Congress Control Number: 99-68454

ISBN 978 1 59114 165 5

First published in the German language under the title *Panzerschiffe der Deutschland-Klasse* by
Bernard & Graefe Verlag, Bonn, 1993
First published in the English language by Greenhill Books, Lionel Leventhal Ltd, 2000

This edition authorized for sale only in the United States of America, its territories and
possessions, and Canada

Translated from the German by Geoffrey Brooks
Printed and bound in China through Printworks International Ltd

Contents

Foreword

The three Panzerschiffe – 'armour-clad ships' – of the *Deutschland* class were the first heavy units to be built by Germany after World War I, and they replaced obsolete pre-dreadnought battleships of the Imperial Navy under the provisions of the 1919 Treaty of Versailles.

The name-ship, *Deutschland*, aroused worldwide interest when she appeared. It had been the purpose of the 1922 Washington Treaty ratified by the victorious sea powers – France, Italy, the United States, Great Britain and Japan – to curtail the massive naval construction programmes pursued by the latter three nations; unintentionally, *Deutschland* overturned the accord and gave impetus to a new naval arms race. As Germany's traditional enemy, France reacted to the 'menace' with the new *Dunkerque* class battleships. Mussolini saw a threat to Italian security from the French and laid down a new class of battleships, to which France responded in turn. Britain was content to look on, but the United States laid down new capital units principally as a precaution in view of Japan's grandiose naval plans.

Of the many beliefs current at one time or another about the Panzerschiffe, the most ludicrous was the allegation voiced at the Nuremberg Trials that the six scheduled, three completed 'pocket battleships' were deliberately designed to spearhead the conquest of the world: rather, they were ships of a hybrid type engineered to fill certain naval roles whilst apparently complying with the letter of the Versailles Treaty, under which it was otherwise impossible for Germany to build a modern, combat-worthy battleship within the tonnage limitations. The design was completely successful even though the hull shape, the arrangement of the armament and, above all, the propulsion machinery were revolutionary in concept.

Pocket Battleships of the Deutschland Class is a companion to two earlier volumes featuring the *Bismarck* and *Scharnhorst* classes. It explains the development stage, provides a detailed review of the important facts and figures and recounts the career history of each vessel separately, supplemented by documentary references, War Diary extracts and combat reports. The text concludes with a critical epilogue. Also provided are detailed sketches, technical tables and a comprehensive selection of photographs not previously published in this compact form, many of which appear in an English-language publication for the first time.

Without the support and assistance of helpers this book could not have been compiled. Valuable references, advice and supporting documents were provided by Werner F. G. Stehr, A. Didrichs and S. Breyer. F. Bavendamm assisted me where necessary with the reproduction of photographs. To all go my grateful thanks.

All plans and sketches were prepared by Klaus-Peter Schmolke unless otherwise stated. Photograph sources were the Town Archive, Wilhelmshaven; the MAN Archive; A. Klein; Renard, Kiel; Urbahns; the U-boat Archive, Cuxhaven; Command Naval Base, North Sea; Marine/Kriegsmarine Werft, Wilhelmshaven; Deutsche Werke, Kiel; the RAF, RN and USN; and PK, Koop Collection/Gally/Klein. Most of the photographs come from my private collection, which comprises the comprehensive stock of photographs bequeathed by the former photographer at the Wilhelmshaven Naval Yard; and from private albums purchased by me from, or from reproductions made from albums lent to me by, former crew members of the three ships.

Gerhard Koop

Introduction

At Jutland in 1916 the German High Seas Fleet proved its hitting power against a superior enemy force, but thereafter it was practically reduced to insignificance. In his diary entry for 7 October 1918, the Fleet Commander-in-Chief, Admiral Hipper, stated that the overriding priority for the Navy was the prosecution of the U-boat war. The duty of the Fleet was to protect the minesweeping formations and the North Sea U-boat bases. This would be achieved by having the Fleet in home waters. Thus the great ships eked out a miserable existence in port or at some secluded anchorage, the monotony broken once or twice by minor forays. The majority of crews, subjected to a negative influence under a leadership riddled with outmoded notions of class, grew to think of themselves as idlers and loafers, and fell an easy prey to the political whisperings of the time. The growing dissatisfaction came to a head with the first mutinies, which were put down ruthlessly. But the mob still seethed with discontent.

Whilst the German Army was bleeding to death in the West, the Fleet remained inactive. Political agitation continued: the naval blockade was starving a war-weary German population into surrender. When the United States was still neutral President Wilson had put forward an alluring 14-point programme for peace. Despite the risk that entering negotiations with the Entente might be interpreted at home as weakness – the United States had since sided with Germany's enemies – the German Government approached the US President as an intermediary in the misguided expectation of obtaining an end to hostilities on fair terms.

In October the situation for Germany was increasingly desperate: on 9 November 1918, at Supreme HQ, Admiral Scheer advised the Kaiser that he could no longer rely on the loyalty of the Fleet. The German Reich accepted an Armistice with conditions which came into effect on 11 November 1918. The Navy was hit very hard. All U-boats, and the most modern sixteen capital ships, eight light cruisers and fifty torpedo-boats of the High Seas Fleet had to be surrendered to the victorious powers. In Germany after the capitulation, revolutionary unrest spread through the surface Navy and the leadership lost its authority vis-ibly. Many officers simply left the Fleet and went home, the men for the most part being no longer willing to serve.

Once the bulk of the Fleet had anchored in Scapa Flow under the Armistice terms, Germany was left with eight capital ships, nineteen old pre-dreadnoughts, eight modern and sixteen old light cruisers and about 120 old torpedo-boats of which most were required to be decommissioned, disarmed and scrapped.

The conditions of the so-called Peace Treaty of Versailles handed down on 7 May 1919 and signed by Germany on 28 June 1919 imposed much harsher terms than expected. Article 181 stipulated that, two months after the Treaty came into force, Germany was limited to having in commission six *Deutschland* or *Lothringen* class pre-dreadnought battleships, six light cruisers, twelve destroyers and twelve torpedo-boats. Any surplus had to be put to reserve or converted to merchant vessels. Article 183 prescribed that the standing naval strength was 15,000 men, of which not more than 10 per cent was to be officer material. U-boats and aircraft were forbidden. The immediate effect of the Treaty was the mass scuttling of the German Fleet on the order of Admiral Reuter on 21 June 1919 in protest. As a reprisal, most of the remaining capital ships and light cruisers remaining in German hands were held forfeit.

On 28 March 1919 the Reichstag had voted through an Act effective from 16 April 1919 for the creation of a 'provisional Reichsmarine'. This was extended upon its expiry on 31 March the following year. On 20 August 1920 the Reich President also proposed the integration of the Navy and Army, but four days later this was turned down by the Reichstag. The Armed Forces Law (Wehrgesetz) of 21 March 1921 provided for six pre-dreadnought battleships and six light cruisers in commission, and two of each in reserve. According to the Treaty, these could not be replaced until twenty years from the anniversary of their launch dates. In 1923, the Reichsmarine had in commission two pre-dreadnought battleships, *Hannover* and *Braunschweig*; five cruisers, *Medusa, Thetis, Berlin, Hamburg* and *Arcona*; 23 torpedo-boats; eleven tenders; the survey ship *Panther*; and the sail training ship *Niobe*. Such was the pitiful state of the Fleet at the time, not only materially but also from the standpoint of personnel. Morale and motivation were at rock-bottom. The numerical limits on the standing Navy imposed by the Treaty allowed the recruiting commissions the opportunity to sift prospective entrants thoroughly, however, while the ranks of serving men were comprehensively purged. The main credit for this was due to the future C-in-C of the Navy, Admiral Raeder.

Development and Construction of the Panzerschiffe

Once the enabling legislation for the provisional Reichsmarine came into force in 1919, the appropriate departments gave thought to the question of how and when a start could be made on building replacements for the obsolete rump of the Fleet. The German economy was in a catastrophic state and the Exchequer faced the burden of making ruinous reparation payments to the victorious powers well into the second half of the twentieth century. Internally the Reich was rent by political turmoil. In the East there were border disputes with Poland. Parts of the Rhineland were under foreign occupation, and in 1923 French and Belgian troops occupied the Ruhr.

Ship types were restricted by the provisions of the Versailles Treaty, and at Government level there were questions as to why Germany needed a Navy. Ultimately the new Reichsmarine owed its existence to the fact that East Prussia had been isolated from the Reich by the unfavourable redrafting of national boundaries in the wake of the defeat, for the connection between Germany proper and the Baltic province was the seaway, and this could only be guaranteed by naval forces.

Up to the building of the light cruiser *Karlsruhe*, all warship construction had been undertaken at the Reichsmarinewerft Wilhelmshaven. The other Imperial Navy Yard (i.e. naval as opposed to private), the Kaiserliche Werft Kiel, had been divided into two unequal parts, the smaller to become the Naval Arsenal and the larger sold into private hands to become the Deutsche Werke Kiel AG, in 1925. These two yards received naval contracts to capacity in order to ensure that their highly qualified workforce of shipbuilders, engine- and boilermakers and weapons specialists was retained intact.

The first new ships built as replacements for existing obsolete units were light cruisers and torpedo-boats, beginning with the light cruiser *Emden* in 1921. The twelve torpedo-boats of the 'Bird/Animal of Prey' class (*Seeadler*, *Luchs*, etc.) appeared in 1924 and were followed in 1925 by the light cruisers *Königsberg*, *Karlsruhe* and *Köln* and in 1927 by *Leipzig*. Additionally, there were various new auxiliaries and training ships.

The provisions of the Versailles Treaty had not been onerous in respect of the size and armament of smaller units such as light cruisers and torpedo-boats, and the major preoccupation in this area was finance.

It was in the field of replacements for the Linienschiffe – pre-dreadnought ships-of-the-line, some of which were 25 years old – that the matter became problematic. Under the Treaty, Germany was allowed to build replacements for existing obsolete units subject to a maximum displacement of 10,000 metric tonnes, the maximum gun calibre not being specified (*Preussen*, a 13,000-tonne Linienschiff eligible for replacement, had a main armament of four 28cm, or 11in, guns). How this could be resolved to Germany's benefit now exercised the minds of Germany's naval planners and architects.

On 6 February 1922 the major naval powers – the United States, Great Britain, France, Italy and Japan – signed the Washington Agreement, the purpose of which was to limit the naval arms race. Germany was not invited to participate in the discussions, even though the restrictions were intended to be universal. The Agreement divided heavy units into two types, capital ships, with a main calibre greater than 20.3cm or 8in, and cruisers, with a maximum calibre of 20.3cm or 8in and a displacement of 10,000 long tons.* The Germans used the ambiguity introduced by the second treaty to design a hybrid warship that had a cruiser's maximum displacement of 10,000 long tons but a small battleship's main armament of at least 28cm, i.e. similar to that of the Linienschiff to be replaced.

Three years of studies preceded the initial secret sketches, and from 1924 another seven versions were produced, these being the basis for eighteen further variations. It was still the major obstacle to find a way to ship all the weight of guns, armour and propulsion machinery more suited to a battleship aboard a 10,000-long ton cruiser hull. The entire responsibility for the task fell to the Head of the Office of Naval Construction, Dr-Ing. h.c. Paul Presse. The urgency of replacing the Linienschiffe is apparent from the steep rise in maintenance costs to 6 million RM in the 1927 fiscal year, of which a quarter went on *Hessen* and *Elsass* alone.

---

* The metric tonne is 1,000kg and the Anglo-American long ton 1,016kg. 10,000 long tons is 11,730m³, displacement weight 11,900 metric tonnes – an increase in displacement of nearly 20 per cent.

Eventually three designs, each having at least some features of the foregoing variations, were submitted to the C-in-C of Naval Command, Admiral Zenker, for a decision on 7 March 1927 –

A 4 × 38cm (15in) guns, 250mm armour, 18kt;
B 6 × 30.5cm (12in) guns, 250 or 200mm armour, 18 or 21kt respectively;
C 6 × 28cm (11in) guns, 100mm armour, 26–27kt.

– all on a 10,000-long ton hull, and on 11 June 1927 Zenker announced that he had decided in favour of Design C. He had the agreement of Vizeadmiral Mommsen, C-in-C Fleet; Vizeadmiral Bauer, C-in-C North Sea Station and Vizeadmiral Raeder, C-in-C Baltic Station, although the last had preferred a monitor type while the three suggestions corresponded to the cruiser type.

At the same time it was decided, in deference to the legal niceties, to classify the new ship as a Panzerschiff, or 'armour-clad ship'. Whereas this was the type description for battleships in the French-language version of the Treaty (Fr. cuirassé = armour-clad ship), Germany had a pre-World War I tradition of Panzerschiffe which were lesser vessels than Linienschiffe. Accordingly, Zenker gave the strictest instructions that the new ships of the type must never be referred to either as battleships or cruisers but simply as 'Panzerschiffe' in conformity with the text of the Treaty.*

At the end of 1927, the Reichsmarine applied for the first instalment of 9.3 million RM to begin construction. Difficulties arose during the Reichstag vote for the appropriation on 17 December 1927. Ministers and deputies were unable to agree on certain aspects and the measure was eventually passed on 27 March 1928, but on the condition that work would not begin on the ship before the end of 1928. Shortly afterwards, Parliament was dissolved and a General Election called for 20 May. During the campaign the subject of the proposed Panzerschiff inspired high feelings on the hustings, the Communist Party being well to the fore in the proceedings with the slogan 'Food for the Children not Panzerkreuzer!' and the left-wing Press (not only Communist periodicals) maintained a strong supporting line. Opposition to the ship spread throughout the SPD, the governing party. Nevertheless, on 10 August 1928 the Cabinet approved the start of construction for 1 September. The SPD itself continued to campaign vigorously, however, and a bill to cancel the building contract was debated on 31 October and defeated by 257 votes to 202. The second instalment for the 1929 fiscal year appropriations was forced through by 224 votes to 153.

This cleared the way at last for Panzerschiff 'A'. The contract was awarded to Deutsche Werke Kiel for mainly social-political reasons. The majority of the Kaiserliche Werft workforce had been laid off at the time of the re-arrangement, and a second bloodletting now threatened the 3,000-strong workforce. The new order saved 1,500 jobs.

The type-sketch as the basis for the design plans had been signed by Zenker and Ministerial Director Presse on 11 April 1928. When the specifications of the German ship became known, the Allies generally were prepared to turn a blind eye, although France protested and obtained authority from the 1930 London Naval Conference to build two Dunkerque class battlecruisers – 35,500 tonnes operational displacement, 8 × 33cm (12.9in) guns, speed 29.5kt – in response.

The Budget appropriations for the second ship – Panzerschiff 'B', the future Admiral Scheer – were not approved by the Reichstag until 1931. Application for a first instalment of 11.75 million RM had been made in 1930: the 1931 instalment was 15.6 million RM, that for 1932 21.55 million RM, and the fourth and final 1933 instalment 24.1 million RM. These amounts were first laid down in the 'Construction Plan for the Replacement of Reichsmarine Warships' agreed on 8 October 1929 but not approved by the Reichstag until 1932.

This plan provided for a series of eight Panzerschiffe by 1940, the displacement of the later versions being steadily increased in stages with, it was hoped, the approval of the victorious powers. The outline details for the design and development of Panzerschiff 'A', launched as Deutschland, were as follows. Length 185.7m oa (181.7m wl) × beam 20.5m oa (20m wl) × draught 5.77m. Displacement 10,000 Imperial tons. Two-shaft diesel drive, maximum output per shaft 54,000 PSe = 53,244hp providing 26kt (2kt forced on trials). Bunkers: 3,000 metric tonnes oil, auxiliary boiler above armour deck. Armament: 6 × 28cm (11in) L/50 guns in triple turrets fore and aft, 8 × 15cm (5.9in) L/55 in centre-pivot gunhouses, 5 × 8.8cm and 4 × 3.7cm Flak, six torpedo tubes in two banks.

Hull and Armour

The proven longitudinal bulkhead/transverse frame system was adhered to for the hull, the internal watertight divisions being further compartmentalised as in the

---

* The first new build vessel to replace the Linienschiff had originally received the label Panzerkreuzer 'A' (= Armoured Cruiser 'A').

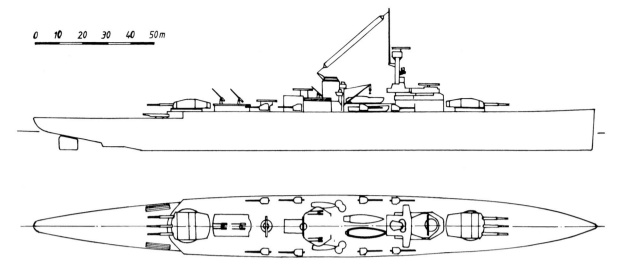

Above: Design sketch for Panzerschiff 'A'

Imperial Navy's shipbuilding tradition. The designers also continued with the electrical arc welding which had been found satisfactory during the Great War, since when the technology had been much improved. One of its advantages was the elimination of rivets, giving a weight saving of about 15 per cent on the hull alone which was passed on to other components, ever with an eye to the 10,000-long ton displacement.

ST52 shipbuilding steel was the principal material used in construction, with ST45 and aluminium for less important fittings. About 90 per cent of the hull and fittings were welded. The double bottom extended for 92 per cent of hull length.

The firm of Krupp supplied a new weldable armour specified as KC (Wotan weak) and KNC (Wotan hard). For less exposed areas nickel-steel armour was used.

The belt armour had an inward 12° slope and provided its protection in combination with a lateral outer bulge from the level of the armoured deck downwards, the wing passage bunker walls serving as torpedo bulkheads. A little further inward, splinter bulkheads rose from the armoured deck to main deck level. As a weight-saving measure the armoured deck covered the beam between the wing passage bunker walls only.

Admiral Scheer was 0.65m beamier than *Deutschland*, some armour thicknesses having been varied. The belt armour was 1m thicker and the barbette armour was increased by 25 per cent to 125mm. This led to an increase in displacement. *Admiral Graf Spee*'s armoured deck covered the full width of the ship and the longitudinal bul-

warks reached to the keel, whereas the double bottom had been considered low enough for the other two ships. The armour of the bulkheads and fighting top was also more substantial. *Graf Spee* displaced 1,740 long tons more than *Deutschland* and 790 long tons more than *Admiral Scheer*. The weight increases in *Scheer* and *Graf Spee* were clear violations of the Versailles Treaty but were legalised retroactively by the 1935 Anglo-German Naval Agreement.

Armament
The various preliminary designs envisaged a main calibre of 38cm (15in), 30.5cm (12in), 28cm (11in) and 21cm (8in), from which 28cm was eventually selected. This was a well-proven gun and had been the standard weapon aboard the World War I battlecruisers *Seydlitz*, *Moltke*, *Goeben* and *Von der Tann* as well as several classes of the later Linienschiffe.

The triple turret arrangement aboard the Panzerschiffe was an innovation for the German Navy. It had been avoided in the past because the centre barrel could not be reloaded when the turret was trained off the centreline amidships and the turret had to be restored to the 0° position after each salvo. The problem had been resolved by adapting the C28 turntable chassis to incorporate a wagon on a circular track at the lower turret platform level which was used to convey the shell to the centre ammunition hoist irrespective of the bearing of the turret. Thus the new turret had a higher rate of fire than the simpler twin gunhouse. The system remained secret until 1945.

The secondary armament was a modernised version of the 15cm (5.9in) weapon which had found favour with the Imperial Navy. The anti-aircraft armament (Flak) was a weak point. Initially, aboard *Deutschland* the inadequate 8.8cm World War I model was fitted. Although exchanged for a newer type of the same calibre, only when the 10.5cm heavy Flak mounting was installed did the anti-aircraft armament correspond to the requirements of the time.

Development History of the Marine Diesel Leading to its Installation aboard the *Deutschland* Class*

The Panzerschiffe were the first heavy units in the world to be equpped with exclusively diesel drive. The engine was the brainchild of Rudolf Diesel.† In his 1893 paper 'Theory and Construction of an Economic Heat Engine to Replace Steam Plant and Current Combustion Engines', he stated that it would eventually prove to be the ideal propulsion system for ships. His opinion was supported by the director of the MAN works at Augsburg, Heinrich Buz, who remarked to an American engineer in 1897 that 'in not so many years even large warships will be driven by diesel motors'.

These predictions were fully realised. The main advantages of marine diesels are: (1) there are no boilers; (2) the engines require less space; (3) all speeds are immediately available (including from stopped) at the push of a button; (4) simplicity of operation, involving no heavy manual labour; (5) lower engine room personnel requirement; (6) economic fuel consumption and greater range; (7) light and clean refuelling; and (8) greater safety in operation. The principal disadvantage of the time was the weight of the unit, but this, as with other types of engine, was merely a question of materials.

In 1905 France had ordered four 300hp four-stroke diesel motors producing 400rpm as propulsion units for two submarines. The unit weight was 33kg/hp. At the same time the Navy Office (Reichsmarineamt) had unsuccessful talks with MAN for the supply of U-boat diesels having a unit weight of 10kg/hp. This was surprising, for by then the motors supplied to France had proved their worth and an experimental 140hp, 400rpm heavy diesel (68kg/hp) installed ashore at the Kaiserliche Werft, Wilhelmshaven, had also found favour.

In 1910 MAN invented a four-stroke, 6-cylinder, 900hp motor with a unit weight of 24kg/hp. During World War I MAN Augsburg supplied a total of 553 four-stroke U-boat diesels of various sizes. The most powerful of these developed 3,000hp.

MAN Nuremberg concentrated on building more powerful two-stroke diesels which seemed to offer the best prospects for progress, particularly for larger warships, the Navy having expressed interest, at a conference at Nuremberg on 25 August 1909, for a large marine diesel which could develop at least 2,000hp. MAN promised experiments towards a 6-cylinder motor of 12,000hp which would be powerful enough to drive a light cruiser. This very ambitious project – until then the largest two-stroke marine diesel was 200hp – occupied the years from 1910 to 1917.

On account of the height of the motor, it was designed to propel the centre shaft of the *Kaiser* class battleship *Prinzregent Luitpold* in combination with two turbine sets on the larger diameter outer propellers. The diesel was a double-acting two-stroke engine with an 850mm diameter cylinder and 1,050mm stroke, producing 160–170rpm. The major difficulties involved materials, but despite this problem the experimental motor, a 3-cylinder unit, ran for the first time on 12 March 1911 and was commissioned on 26 March. Its initial output of 3,000hp was later increased to 5,400 hp at 90 per cent of its designed efficiency. Approval for the construction of the whole engine was granted after the test motor gave no problems during a nine-day trial in June 1913.

A 6-cylinder motor started on 23 February 1914 had registered an output in excess of 10,000hp at 150rpm that September, but by then World War I was interfering with progress. A shortage of fuel forced the manufacturers to resort to the use of coal-tar oil. The first experiments with this substitute were tried with a single-cylinder engine on 17 April 1915, followed by successful 72-hour and five-day runs at 2,130hp and 2,030hp respectively, after which the oil was used to fuel even the 6-cylinder diesel. Further cylinders were built, but only in January 1917 were fresh trials held, the efficiency increasing steadily: 5 March (12-hour run, 128rpm),10,000hp; 18 March (130rpm), 10,800 hp = 90% of designed efficiency; and finally 24 March (12-hour run, 135rpm), 12,200hp.

The official acceptance trials began on 31 March, the diesel being required to achieve 10,800hp at 130rpm on a five-day run. On 1 April, over a 12-hour period, an output of 12,400hp was achieved using a fuel mixture of coal-tar oil/paraffin in the ratio 214:29 at 243g/hp/hr.

---

* Unless otherwise stated, the German term 'PSe' (effective Pferdestärke = diesel horsepower) has been converted to standard hp throughout this volume. 1 PSe = 75 kgm/s = 0.9860hp.
† Rudolf Diesel, born Paris of German parents 1858, drowned 1913 (allegedly fell overboard from Antwerp–Harwich steamer on a business visit to Britain).

Thus, after a six-year development phase, the diesel was ready for installation aboard ship, but the Navy was not prepared to withdraw *Prinzregent Luitpold* from the line for a refit and the engine was eventually scrapped ashore at the war's end. A diesel of similar type was also built by the Krupp-owned Germania Werft, Kiel. Initially it was planned to install a diesel plant aboard all four battleships (later only *Grosser Kurfürst* and *Markgraf*) of the *König* class, and *Sachsen*, the last of the *Bayern* class to be launched, but nothing came of these schemes.

The immediate postwar period brought even the large engine manufacturers to the verge of bankruptcy. The victorious powers required the handing over of all U-boat diesels amd imposed daunting regulations to inhibit the development and production of certain diesel types, but by mid-1926 MAN Augsburg had managed to start work on an extremely light double acting two-stroke motor (piston diameter 230mm, piston stroke 340mm, 250hp per cylinder at 800rpm, ignition pressure 5.2kg/cm^2, unit weight not exceeding 5kg/hp) for the propulsion of warships up to about torpedo-boat size. Little is known about the development history because all correspondence, designs and blueprints were classified 'highly secret', close contact being maintained at all times between the MAN Senior Design Engineer G. Pielstik and the Senior Ministerial Adviser at the Reichsmarineamt, Wilhelm Laudahn.

On 14 August 1926 MAN offered the Navy a diesel consisting of four 12-cylinder units each producing 250hp with two 3-cylinder auxiliaries of a size sufficient to drive a torpedo-boat. On 28 August the Navy placed an order, subject to a satisfactory 72-hour test-run by June 1927. MAN began work at once on the development (motor D4Z 23/24). Although good results had been obtained with four-stroke motors of another series, and also with the direct-injection type WV26/33, air injection was designed for the new type and proved unsatisfactory on the test stand during the second half of 1927. By now the trend towards compressorless drive was almost irresistible, but it was the autumn of 1928 before an experimental direct-injection motor was ready. The Reichsmarine had rescinded the contract before then on the grounds of the repeated teething problems and replaced it on 27 March 1928 with an order for an auxiliary cruising diesel for the planned 'Cruiser E' (the later *Leipzig*), the keel of which had not yet been laid. Previously the new cruisers *Königsberg*, *Karlsruhe* and *Köln* had been fitted with MAN cruising diesels, but these were fast-running four-stroke engines of series W10 V26/30 used to turn both shafts once the steam turbine drive had been uncoupled –

progress certainly, but a complicated procedure nonetheless. The intention for *Leipzig* was for three shafts, the diesel driving the centre shaft only once the outer shaft had been uncoupled.

Up to the time of delivery, barely three years had elapsed since the initial design: in October 1928 the Reichsmarine ordered the diesel plant for Panzerkreuzer 'A' (the later *Deutschland*), followed on 9 January 1930 by that for the gunnery training ship *Bremse* then on the stocks. The contract for the *Admiral Scheer* diesel was placed on 14 March 1931 and for *Admiral Graf Spee*'s the following year.

It has been assumed in the past that the *Bremse* diesel was an experimental prototype for the Panzerschiff motors. However the diesels aboard *Deutschland* were ordered much earlier and were not of the same type; the engine arrangement was similar, but *Bremse* had only half the number of units. This erroneous assumption arose because *Bremse* entered service before *Deutschland*. The diesel units aboard *Bremse* and *Leipzig* were blighted from the beginning, and not until the end of 1939 had the faults been more or less ironed out. Modifications to the Panzerschiff engines were made during construction on the basis of reports from other units, and one of these modifications was a reduction in engine revolutions, but nevertheless serious problems were experienced, particularly in respect of the crossheads and drive rods. These weaknesses were gradually eliminated during regular shipyard checks. Other vulnerable areas were the suspension vibration absorbers and, worst of all, the motor rooms themselves where the motor foundations and floors were defective. The cause of this was the the Reichsmarine's contractural condition for light construction, which in turn had its origins in the displacement limit set by the Versailles Treaty. By the time Panzerschiff C' was on the stocks, these defects had been taken into account.

A design peculiarity was the sacrifice of a cast-iron chassis for sheet metal and bearers welded together, foundation plates being replaced by through bolts. Other major problems eventually overcome included the delivery of exhaust fumes into the motor room by the ventilation system and intolerable noise levels in the exhaust piping.

Summary

The three Panzerschiffe, as diesel-driven capital ships, were the culmination of a unique technical endeavour first embarked upon prior to World War I. Strategic considerations were surely behind the idea, since a diesel engine was unnecessary for operational use in the North Sea and Baltic, coal being always on hand in German ports for coal-fired units. Oil for steam-turbine and diesel-driven warships was, naturally, vastly more convenient but had to be imported – and Germany was easy to blockade by sea.

Since time immemorial, Germany's traditional enemy had been her neighbour France, and France was very dependent on imports. She was a large colonial power and therefore had a powerful navy, with fleets in the Mediterranean (to meet the possible Italian threat) and the Atlantic (as a precaution against Great Britain and, more particularly, a reawakening Germany). In addition, she had sea trade routes to protect to and from her overseas territories.

To attack these lines of supply, German steam-driven capital ships and cruisers were unsuitable to roam the oceans: the diesel-driven Panzerschiff was the answer. With their heavy armament, light armour and long range, the *Deutschland* class made ideal commerce raiders, and when first seen by the major sea powers they caused consternation. On the one hand, they overturned the intention of the 1922 Washington Treaty to limit warship size, since the legal draughtsmen had not speculated on possible hybrid developments of this nature. In a long article appraising *Deutschland* published on 23 June 1933 in the *Naval Engineering Journal*, the organ of the Society of American Naval Engineers, the writer stated: 'It is an indisputable fact that the USA is now so hamstrung by Treaty provisions that the nation is no longer in a position to build ships of a type to neutralise the *Deutschland* even if she offered a present threat. We have practically abandoned our right to self-protection, even in those areas where strength is indispensable for our national survival.' On the other hand, the Panzerschiffe were 10,000-ton cruisers with armour thin enough to enable them to carry a battleship's guns. The former C-in-C of the Fleet Division, Konteradmiral von Loewenfeld, first described the ideal blend of warship as one which 'was faster than any ship more powerful, and more powerful than any faster ship'. The French were the first to recognise the danger and responded with the two faster and more powerful battlecruisers of the *Dunkerque* class as a countermeasure. Nevertheless, the three Panzerschiffe were far ahead of their time: previously only the British battlecruisers *Hood*, *Renown* and *Repulse* had been both faster and stronger. But these British and French units could not be everywhere at once, and two-thirds of the world's surface is ocean: *Admiral Scheer* proved in her long commerce raiding voyage that a Panzerschiff could operate for months and remain undiscovered. However, the flaw in Konteradmiral von Loewenfeld's remarks was amply demonstrated by the plight of *Admiral Graf Spee* during and after the Battle of the River Plate: they did not necessarily hold good in a battle against faster, lighter-armed opponents who could not be shaken off.

The various sea powers viewed the development of the Panzerschiff with a range of critical observations from deprecation to admiration. The jocular term 'pocket-battleship' was coined by the British technical press, at a loss how to classify the new type.

Below: A broadside view of *Admiral Graf Spee* prior to her 1938 refit.

Data

Sources: Gröner, Witte, Whitley and official documents.
All weights hereunder are expressed in metric tonnes unless otherwise stated.

	Deutschland	*Admiral Scheer*	*Admiral Graf Spee*
Builder	Deutsche Werke Kiel	Marinewerft Wilhelmshaven	Marinewerft Wilhelmshaven
Yard number	219	123	124
Building costs (RM)	80m	90m (plus 6.4m for conversion)	82m
Official displacement (long tons)	10,000	10,000	10,000
Actual displacement (long tons)	10,600	11,550 (after conversion)	12,340
Standard displacement	12,630	13,660	14,890
Operational displacement, max.	14,290	15,180	16,320
Length wl (m)	181.7	181.7	181.7
Length oa before conversion (m)	186.0	186.0	186.0
Length oa after conversion (m)	187.9	187.9	
Beam (m)	20,69	21.34	21.65
Draught (m)	5.78	5.78	5.80
Operational draught (m)	7.25	7.25	7.34
Measurement (brt)	9,402 as *Lützow*	9,445	9,596
Measurement (nrt)			6,299
Machinery output at 250rpm (PSe)	48,390/54.000	52,050/54,000	54,000
Speed (kt)	26–28	26–28.3	26–28.5
Range (nm/kt)	10,000/20 16,600/14 17,400/13	9,100/20	8,900/20
Bunkerage (m³)	2,750	2,410	2,500
Height of sides (m)	12.4	12.2	12.2
Watertight compartments	XVI	XVI	XVI
Shipboard aircraft	2	2	2
Ship's boats	7 (later 5)	8	10
Searchlights	5	6 (later 5)	6 (later 5)
Crew (ten divisions)	Peacetime complement 33 officers and 586 men From 1935: 30 officers and 921–1,040 men As Fleet flagship: + 17 officers and 85 men As flagship BdP*: + 13 officers and 59 men From 1939: + war supplementary intake, variable strengths later depending upon operational deployment and number of light AA carried		

* BdP = Befehlshaber der Panzerschiffe (C-in-C Panzerschiffe).

CONSTRUCTION GROUPINGS FOR *ADMIRAL GRAF SPEE* (per Witte)

Length cwl (construction waterline) (m)	181.7
Beam cwl (m)	21.7
Height of side (m)	9.95
Construction draught	6.5
Machinery output unforced (PSe)	56,000
Maximum speed (kt)	27
Ship's company	1,150
Building steel	ST 52
Main armament	6 × 28cm
Secondary armament	8 × 15cm
AA armament (exc. machine guns)	6 × 10.5cm
Torpedo battery	2 × 4
Aircraft	2
Armour thickness, max. (mm) (deck)	70
(sides)	100
Range at cruising speed (nm/kt)	10,000/19

Weight Grouping (tonnes)

Individual construction groups have an identification letter used initially for calculation purposes in the design stages but ultimately retained throughout the period of the ship's useful life.

S = Weight of compartmented hull, comprising S I (building materials, e.g. steel ST 52, excluding waterline armour), S II (metalworkers), S III (carpenters), S IV (painters).

M I = Main machinery and connections, condensers, gear couplings, shaft connections, propellers, auxiliary machinery, conduits and piping used in connection with the operation of the main machinery, exhaust/funnel cap, equipment, etc., boilers with armatures, oil and water in the main engine plant.

M II = Auxiliary boiler plant, ship's heating system, washing and drinking water desalination plant, laundry, ablutions, kitchen gear etc., ship's pumps, primary electrical plant, lighting, cables, steering assembly, capstans, boats' windlasses, room fans, weapon systems, refrigerating plant, searchlights, signal lamps, command elements, gyro compass, mileage logs, sirens and workshops.

Weights		
	S I–S IV, inc. armour	3,984
	Ship's gear, supplies, crew and effects, provisions and fresh water	1,070
	Armour, less turrets	2,821
	Main machinery plant with equipment (M I)	1,678
	Fuel, lubricating oil	3,292

Auxiliary machinery and equipment (M II)	760
Armament and equipment, plus ammunition	2,715
Full load displacement	16,320
Designed displacement	14,207

Weight Distribution (%)

Ship's hull	26.4
Armour	41.7
M I	7.1
M II	3.0
Weapons and aircraft	15.2
Instruments and supplies, crew, effects and provisions	2.0
Potable and washing water	1.0
Fuel	3.6

WEIGHT GROUPINGS FOR *ADMIRAL GRAF SPEE* (per Witte)

Total weight for S = 6,805t

S I	=	3984t (building steel ST45 and ST52)
S I	=	2 821t (armour less turrets plus barbettes)
S II	=	284t (metal workers)
S III	=	86t (carpenters)
S IV	=	70t (painters)

In another analysis (t):

Ship's hull	3,984
Armour, less turrets	2,821
Main machinery (inc. equipment)	1,648
Auxiliary machinery (inc. equipment)	760
Guns (inc. equipment)	2,042
Torpedo batteries (inc. equipment)	60
Aircraft installation (inc. equipment)	26
Mines (inc. equipment)	3
General equipment	200
Nautical equipment	10
Masts and rigging	10
Ballast and anti-roll installation	164
Empty ship with equipment	11,458
Ammunition	562
Torpedoes	21
Mines	1
Aircraft ammunition	–
Supplies	25

Crew		97
Effects		70
Provisions		40
Type displacement (exc. potable and washing water)		12,546
Potable water		91
Washing water		110
Boiler feedwater		36
Heating oil		70
Diesel oil		1,225
Lubricating oil		83
Aviation spirit		8
Construction displacement		14,207
Feedwater		40
Heating oil		40
Diesel oil		1,467
Lubricating oil		84
Aviation spirit		–
Reserve fresh water		253
Operational displacement		16,320

COEFFICIENTS OF FORM AT DISPLACEMENT OF 11,910 TONNES (per Witte)

Ratio length cwl/beam	8.8
Ratio beam/draught	3.58
Longitudinal prismatic coefficient (δ)	0.53
Coefficient, fineness of waterplane (α)	0.68
Ratio (δ/α)	0.79
Midship section coefficient (β)	0.89
Ratio (δ/β)	0.60

Uniform trim moment: *Deutschland* 23,060m⁴/m
Admiral Scheer 22,056m⁴/m
Admiral Graf Spee 22,661m⁴/m

Note: The longitudinal prismatic coefficient is the ratio of the volume of displacement to the volume of a prism having a length equal to the length between perpendiculars and a cross-sectional area equal to the midship sectional area. The fineness of waterplane coefficient is the ratio of the area of the waterplane to the area of its circumscribing rectangle. The midship section coefficient is the ratio of the midship section area to the area of a rectangle whose sides are equal to the draught and breadth extreme amidships. The foregoing values of form were approximately the same for all three ships.

Comparison of the M I and M II Weights (tonnes)

	Deutsch-land	Admiral Scheer	Admiral Graf Spee
M I (in tonnes)			
Diesel motors	900.010	981.980	1,013.083
Drive, couplings	61.386	60.738	56.498
Piping	36.713	67.347	109.273
Shafts	184.864	158.671	158.811
Propellers	26.483	27.092	27.159
Ventilation installations	19.672	11.760	11.765
Decking and floor plating	15.295	24.042	20.487
Cables	9.998	14.380	21.758
Tools	6.056	3.240	4.308
Equipment	55.784	55.232	62.318
Total	1316.261	1412.852	1482.868
Fuel (in piping)	102.900	232.000	230.500
M II (in tonnes)			
Total	559.052	6653.289	761.677
M I + M II total	1978.213	2308.141	2475.045

Below: A photograph of the lower level of one of the main diesel rooms – the normal watch station – aboard *Admiral Graf Spee.*

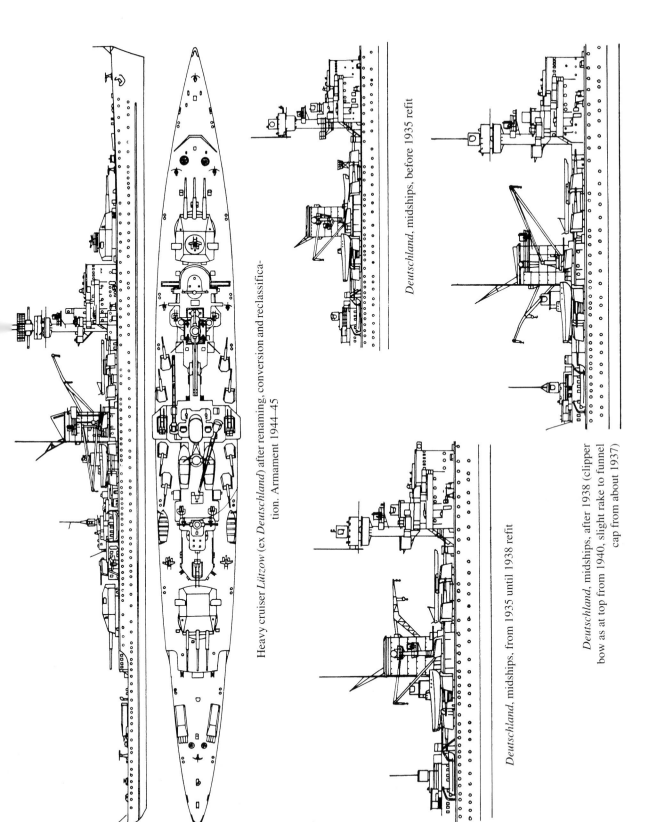

Heavy cruiser *Lützow* (ex *Deutschland*) after renaming, conversion and reclassification. Armament 1944-45

Deutschland, midships, before 1935 refit

Deutschland, midships, from 1935 until 1938 refit

Deutschland, midships, after 1938 (clipper bow as at top from 1940, slight rake to funnel cap from about 1937)

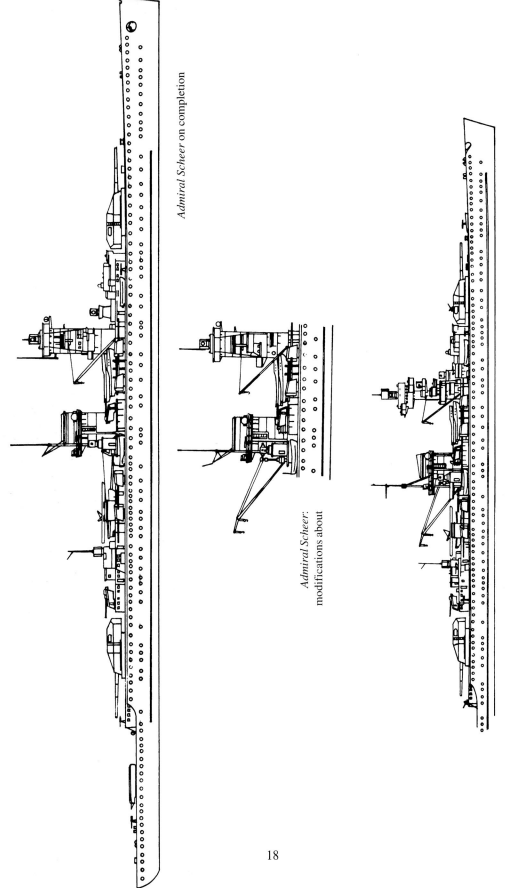

Admiral Scheer on completion

Admiral Scheer:
modifications about

Admiral Scheer: appearance after conversion and reclassification as heavy cruiser, 1940

Admiral Scheer: modifications about 1944

Admiral Scheer: plan view, 1945

Admiral Graf Spee at the outbreak of war, 1939

Armour

All data in millimetres

	Deutschland	Admiral Scheer	Admiral Graf Spee
Vertical armour:			
Belt armour inclined inwards about 12°			
upper	80	50	80
lower	60	80	
fore and aft	60	partly behind bulges and 1m broader, fore 17, aft 50	
stern	50–30		
foreship	10		10
Armoured bulkheads			
fore and aft	60	40 and 50	100
Longitudinal splinter bulkheads	10	40	40
Wing passage (torpedo) bulkheads	45	40	40
Horizontal armour:			
Upper deck	18	17	17
Armoured deck	30–45	40	
within the citadel		45	20
betw. wing passage and splinter longitudinal bulkhead			40
betw. wing passage bulkhead and outer plating			30
forecastle and stern	30		
Armour in region of rudder gear:			
sides	30	45–50	
deckhead	30	45	
connecting bulkhead			45
Command centre fwd:			
sides	140	150	150
roof	50	50	50
companionway	60	60	60
Command centre aft:			
sides	60	50	50
Foretop:			
sides	14	60	60
roof	14	20	20
Rangefinder domes	20	20	20
28cm turrets: face	140	140	140
sides	75–80	75–80	75–85
roof	50–105	50–105	90–105
rear wall	170	170	170
Barbettes	125	125	125
15cm gun shields	10	10	10

ARMOUR DISTRIBUTION: *DEUTSCHLAND*

Armour, vertical and/or horizontal		Thickness (mm)	Material
Frame	6.5–16	30	Nickel steel
	16–25.75	40	Nickel steel
	25.75–31	50	Nickel steel
	31–42.4	60	Nickel steel
	42.4–136.4	50–80	Nickel steel
	136.4–154	60	Nickel steel
	154–forepeak	18	Nickel steel
28cm turrets:			
face		140	KC

side (fwd part)	80	KC
side (rear part)	75	KNC
rear wall	170	Nickel steel
roof (above face)	105	KC
roof (to rear wall)	85	KNC/KC
roof (rear end)	50	KNC
roof (twds face)	90	KNC
Turret bed amid.		
fore	80	KNC
face and rear wall	30	KNC
sides	60	KNC
Barbettes:		
plating	100	KC
shoring	30	Special steel
Command tower (command centre fwd):		
7m r/finder dome	55	Nickel steel
roof	50	Nickel steel
side plates	140	KC
bed	30	Nickel steel
companionway	60	Nickel steel
deck plating	10	SB Steel III
Command centre aft:		
roof	20	Ww n/A
deck plating	20	Ww n/A
walls	50	Wh n/A
Foretop: Main gunnery control centre, roof, deck and walls	14	Ww n/A
Rangefinder rotating dome aft:		
roof, deck	20	Ww n/A
walls	50	Ww n/A
Foretop rangefinder rotating dome:		
roof, deck, walls	14	Ww n/A
Flak control centres, fore and aft:		
roof and walls	14	Ww n/A
Searchlight control centres	10	SB Steel II

Splinter protection for 8.8cm and 3.7cm Flak ammunition hoists	20	Nickel steel
Splinter protection for pipework	10	Wh n/A
Torpedo (wing-passage) bulkhead	45	Nickel steel
Lateral splinter protection from armoured deck to superstructure and between two main 28cm gun turrets	10	SB Steel II
Armoured transverse bulkheads:		
Frame 6.5	30	Nickel steel
Frame 31	60	Nickel steel
Frame 149.5	60	Nickel steel
Frame 173.5	30	Nickel steel
Decks: armoured deck inside wing-passage bulkhead	30	Nickel steel
armoured deck beyond wing-passage bulkhead	45	Nickel steel
armoured deck inside barbettes	15	Nickel steel
armoured deck between Frames 6.5 and 31	30	Nickel steel
armoured deck betw. Frames 149.5 and 173.5	30	Nickel steel
'tween deck betw. Frames 31 and 149.5 outside armoured deck	20	SB Steel II
superstructure deck betw. Frames 33 and 154	18	SB Steel III
superstructure deck to Frame 164.5	10	SB Steel III
superstructure deck from Frame 164.5	7	SB Steel III

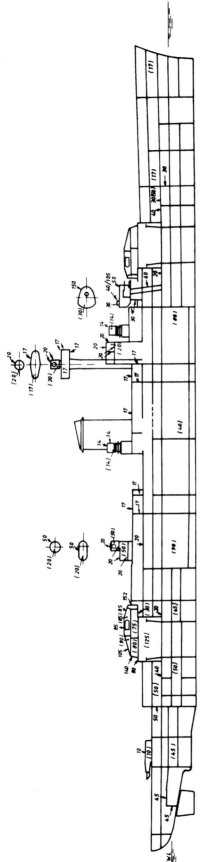

Admiral Scheer: armour distribution after conversion to heavy cruiser (values in parentheses show vertical thicknesses of armour)

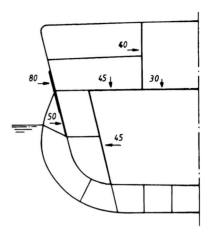

Deutschland/Lützow: main frame

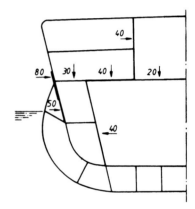

Admiral Graf Spee: main frame

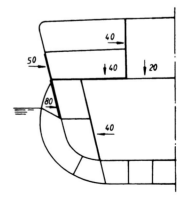

Deutschland/Lützow: main frame

Notes on Armour Materials

The nickel content of nickel steel was approximately 4 per cent (per Vol. 8, No. 29, *Materials Specification*, 1915).

KC = Krupp cemented, a weldable, surface-hardened steel with a carbon content of 0.37% (old) to 0.34% (new), nickel 4.10% (old) to 3.78% (new), manganese 0.30% (old) to 0.31% (new) and chrome from 1.89% (old) to 2.06% (new).

KNC = Krupp non-cemented, a weldable, non-hardened steel.

Special steel was an alloy (per Vol. 8, No 15, *Materials Specification*, 1915).

SB (Shipbuilding) Steel III (S III) was developed in about 1906. Shipbuilding Steel ST 52 was a further development specified in 1933 at 50–62kg/mm^2 ultimate tensile strength, 34–36 kg/mm^2 expansion and with a yield point at 18–20%. S III had had an ultimate tensile strength of 2 kg/mm^2.

SB (Shipbuilding) Steel II was developed from about 1901 for shipboard protection in areas not immediately vulnerable to splinter damage. Shipbuilding Steel ST 42 was a further development of this material with the following specifications: 41–48 kg/mm^2 ultimate tensile strength, 24kg/mm^2 expansion and with a yield point of 18–22% (per Vol. 8, Nos. 16 and 26, *Materials Specification*). S II and S III were further stages of Steel S I, which had been first manufactured in 1901 for splinter protection in highly vulnerable areas such as outer plating, side armour, superstructure and upper deck.

Wh n/A ('wotan hard') and Ww n/A ('wotan-weich' = 'wotan soft') were further developments of KNC steel, weldable with a special electrode. The values were 85–95kg/mm^2 ultimate tensile strength, 50–55kg/mm^2 expansion and yield point 20% (wotan hard); and 65–75kg/mm^2 ultimate tensile strength, 38–40kg/mm^2 expansion and 25% yield point (wotan soft).

Below: A photograph of *Admiral Graf Spee* taken from a security boat showing crewmen suspended over the side in boatswain's chairs and engaged in the routine task of sprucing up the paintwork. Above them, on the upper deck and superstructure, the 'steamer' is being made ship-shape. The belt armour is prominent on this illustration.

Armament

Main: 6 × 28cm SK L/52 C28 in two triple C28 turrets with roller track platform*

Secondary: 8 × 15cm SK L/55 C28 in C28 centre-pivotal gunhouses

Flak:† 3 × 8.8cm C13 centre-pivotal housing (*Deutschland* only): from 1934/1935 replaced by 6 × 8.8cm Flak L/75 C32 on triaxially stabilised twin mounting C31, these being replaced later by 6 × 10.5cm Flak L/65 C33 on the existing 8.8cm C31 chassis.
8 × 3.7cm Flak L/83 C30 in twin mountings C30.
8 × 2cm Flak L/65 C30 on centre-pivotal chassis C30.

Later aboard *Admiral Scheer* the 3.7cm Flak was exchanged for single-mounted 4cm Bofors 28 and additionally 2 × 2cm Flak C38 with Flak-sight 35. The total of 2cm weapons aboard *Admiral Scheer* was continually augmented and eventually included 28 2cm barrels in four quadruple and six twin mountings. At the war's end she had 8 × 3.7cm and 33 × 2cm barrels. For her commerce-raiding cruise *Admiral Graf Spee* was equipped with 12 × 2cm Flak. At the war's end *Lützow* (ex *Deutschland*) carried a Flak armament of 6 × 4cm Bofors 28, 10 × 3.7cm and 28 × 2cm.

Torpedoes 8 × 53.3cm (*Deutschland* 50cm) TTs in two quadruple banks.

DESCRIPTION OF INDIVIDUAL WEAPONS

28cm (11in) Gun

Description	28cm SK L/52 C28 on C28 roller track platform
Calibre	283mm
Barrel length	52.35cal/14.815m
Bore length	49.13cal/13.905m
Muzzle velocity	910 m/sec
Barrel life	340 rounds
Length of grooving:	11.41m

Number of grooves	80 (3.25mm deep and 6.72mm broad)
Length of breech chamber	2.333m
Volume of breech chamber	160dm³
Chamber pressure	3.2tonnes/cm²
Weight of barrel and breech	48.2 tonnes
Turret turning weight	600 tonnes
Maximum range	36.475km at 40° elevation
Maximum elevation/depression	+40°/–10°; barrel loaded at 2°
Rate of fire	2 rounds/min
Ammunition stock per turret	315–360 rounds

Projectiles and Powder

AP shell L/3.7, wt 300kg, length 1.047m, explosive charge 7.84kg = 2.6% with base fuze 38.

HE shell L/4.2, wt 300kg, length 1.188m, explosive charge 16.94kg = 5.65% with base fuze 38.

HE shell L/4.2, wt 300kg, length 1.188m, explosive charge 23.33kg = 7.8% with nose fuze 27.

Main cartridge case (metal), wt 189.5kg, propellant 71kg RPC 38‡

Additional propellant (bag) wt 36kgs, propellant 36kgs RPC 38.

Aboard German warships prior to the outbreak of war, the explosive was virtually always TNT. Later this was replaced by Hexogen, TNT with 5% beeswax and wax additive. Related to 1kg, the explosion temperature was 3,800°C

---

* SK = Schnell-lade/Schnellfeuerkanone (quick-loading/quick-firing gun). L is the length of the gun barrel expressed in multiples of the calibre. Thus 28cm/L52 = a barrel length of 14.56m.
† The term Flak, a contraction of Fliegerabwehrkanone, is used throughout this book to describe AA (anti-aircraft) weapons and installations both aboard ship and ashore.
‡ RPC38 = Rauchpulver 1938, powder and its year of introduction.

and the specific volume 880 litres, corresponding to 13,129 litres with a detonation speed of 8,500 m/sec and a gas pressure of 143,000 kgs/cm^2. The total amount of gas was in consequence variable.

Below: The triple turrets of the *Deutschland* class: 28cm SK L/52 C28 on roller track chassis C28 ('A' turret shown).

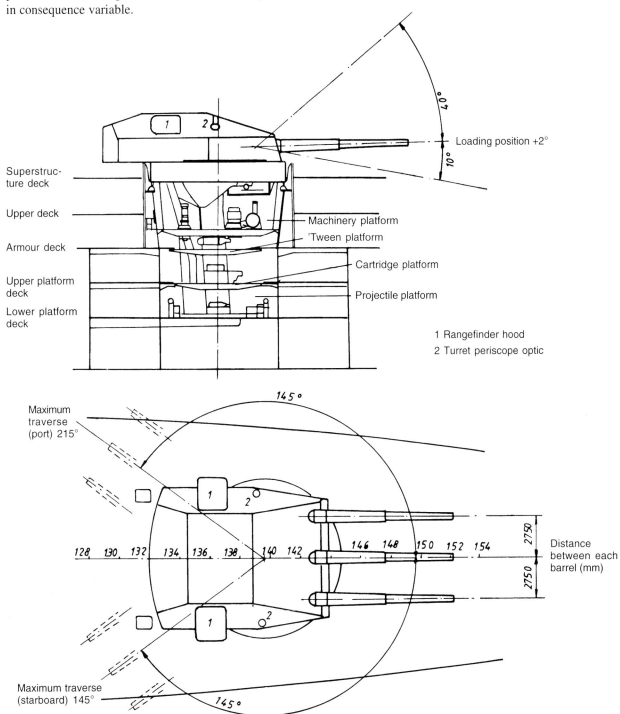

Loading position +2°

Superstructure deck

Upper deck

Armour deck

Upper platform deck

Lower platform deck

Machinery platform
'Tween platform
Cartridge platform
Projectile platform

1 Rangefinder hood
2 Turret periscope optic

Maximum traverse (port) 215°

Maximum traverse (starboard) 145°

Distance between each barrel (mm)

128 130 132 134 136 138 140 142 146 148 150 152 154

Range (m)	Barrel elevation (°)	Angle of descent (°)	Impact velocity (m/s)
5,000	1.9	2.4	752
10,000	4.5	6.0	611
15,000	8.0	11.8	493
20,000	12.5	21.4	407
25,000	18.6	34.2	360
30,000	26.3	46.4	363
35,000	36.4	56.0	380

Below: Characteristics of 28cm SK C28 shell of weight 300kg and V_0 910 m/s

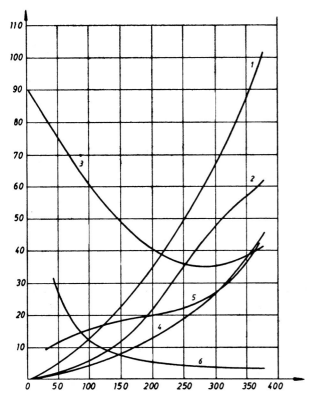

Key: (1) Flight time in seconds. (2) Impact angle. (3) Terminal velocity in dm/sec. (4) Barrel elevation in degrees. (5) Probability of error in dm. (6) Scatter in dm.
Note: A decametre (dm) is 10 metres. The range is expressed in hectometres, tenths of a kilometre, the usual range measurement factor in German gunnery. To avoid confusion, ranges have generally been expressed as kilometres and parts of a kilometre elsewhere in this book.

15cm Gun

Description	15cm SK/L55 C28 on centre-pivotal chassis C28
Calibre	149.1mm
Barrel length	55cal/8.20m
Length of barrel lining	52.5cal/7.816m
Muzzle velocity (V_0)	875m/sec
Barrel life	1,100 rounds/barrel
Designed gas pressure	3,050kg/cm^2
Recoil energy at 0° elevation	52 tonnes
Maximum range	22,000m at 35° barrel elevation
Maximum elevation/ depression	+35°/–10°
Length of grooving	6,588m
Type of grooving	Cubic parabola 50/30cal
Number of grooves	44
Wt of barrel with breech	9.026t
Rate of fire	10 rounds/min

Ammunition

Wt of projectile	45.3kg
Wt of charge	3,058–3,892kg
Filling	Fp 02
Projectile length	4.5cal/0.655m , 4.6cal/0.67789m
Wt of cartridge case	23.5kg
Length of cartridge case	0.865m
Propellant	RPC 32
Fuze type	C 27
Ammunition supply	100–150 rounds/gun.

Chassis

Rotation speed	1.04° per turn (hand-elevated), 8°/sec (powered)
Rotation speed	1.09° per turn (by hand), 9°/sec (powered)

8.8cm Flak

Description	8.8cm Flak L/45 on centre-pivotal chassis C13
Calibre	88mm
Muzzle velocity (V_0)	79m/sec
Recoil energy	13.2 tonnes
Wt of gun and breech	2.5 tonnes
Wt of projectile	9kg

Wt of charge	2.35kg
Maximum elevation/	
depression	+70°/–10°

Note: This World War I weapon was fitted aboard *Deutschland* only and later replaced.

8.8cm Flak

The 8.8cm Flak L/75 twin C25, intended to replace the World War I Flak, was tested aboard the 'K' class light cruisers and found to be unsatisfactory. The Panzerschiffe therefore received an improved model.

Description	8.8cm SK/L76 C32 in triaxially stabilised double chassis C31
Calibre	88mm
Barrel length	76cal/6.69m
Length of barrel lining	72cal/6.34m
Muzzle velocity (V_0)	950m/sec
Designed gas pressure	3,150kg/cm²
Recoil energy at 0° elevation	7.8 tonnes
Barrel life	3,200 rounds
Wt of barrel and breech	3.640 tonnes
Maximum range	17,200m surface target; 12,400m ceiling

Ammunition

Wt of projectile	9kg
Wt of charge	3.1kg
Length of projectile	39.7cm
Wt of whole shell	15kg
Length of whole shell	93.2cm

Chassis

Maximum barrel elevation/depression	+80°/–10°
Rotation speed of chassis	2.5°/sec
Rotation speed for barrel elevation	3.6°/sec by hand, 10°/sec powered
Wt of gun cradle	1.775 tonnes
Wt of gun bedding	0.815 tonne
Wt of chassis	6.257 tonnes
Wt of sights	0.745 tonne
Wt of electric motor	1.280 tonnes
Wt of protective shield	5.830 tonnes
Total weight	23.650 tonnes

10.5cm Flak

Eventually the three ships received a 10.5cm AA battery to replace the 8.8cm guns but retaining the chassis.

Description	10.5cm SK/L65 C33 on 8.8cm twin chassis C31
Calibre	105mm
Barrel length	65cal/6.84m
Length of barrel lining	60.5cal/6.348m
Muzzle velocity (V_0)	900m/sec
Designed gas pressure	2,850kg/cm²
Recoil energy	1.3 tonnes
Barrel life	2,950 rounds/barrel
Length of grooving	5.53m
Type of grooving	Cubic parabola 55/35cal
Number of grooves	16
Weight of barrel and breech	243kg
Maximum range	17,700m surface target; 12,500m ceiling at 80° elevation

Ammunition

Weight of projectile	15.1kg
Weight of charge	5.2kg
Propellant	Fp 02
Projectile length	45.9cm (L4.4) as HE, 43.8cm (4.0) as tracer
Weight of cartridge case	6kg
Length of cartridge case	76.9cm
Propellant	C32
Fuze	S 30 (time), S 6 (tracer)
Total shell weight	26.5kg (normal), 23.5kg (tracer)
Total length	1.163m (normal), 1.142m (tracer)

Chassis

Maximum elevation/depression:	+80°/–8°
Barrel elevation	1.33°/sec per rev. by hand, 10°/sec powered
Rotation speed	1.5°/sec by hand, 8°/sec powered
Wt of gun cradle	1.455 tonnes
Wt of gun bed	2.3 tonnes
Wt of chassis	7.15 tonnes
Wt of sights	0.745 tonne
Wt of electric motor	1.295 tonnes
Wt of protective shield	6.13 tonnes
Total weight	27.35 tonnes

3.7cm Flak

Description	3.7cm SK L/83 C30 on twin chassis C30
Calibre	37mm
Barrel length	83cal/3.074m
Length of bore	80cal/2.960m
Muzzle velocity (V_0)	1,000m/sec
Muzzle energy	38 megatonnes
Designed gas pressure	3,450kg/cm^2
Barrel life	7,500 rounds/barrel
Recoil energy at 0° elevation:	1 tonne
Length of grooving	2.554m
Type of grooving	Cubic parabola 50/35cal
Number of grooves	16
Wt of barrel and breech	243kg
Maximum range	8,500m surface target, 6,800m ceiling at 80° elevation, 4,800m tracer

Ammunition

Weight of projectile	0.742kg
Weight of charge	0.365kg
Propellant	Fp 02
Length of projectile	16.2cm
Wt of cartridge case	0.97kg
Length of cartridge case	38.1cm
Propellant	RPC 32
Total shell wt	2.1kg
Fuze	C 30 (time), C 34 (impact), ErsSt C 34 (tracer)
Duration of tracer illumination	12sec
Rate of fire	160 rounds/barrel/min (in theory) 80 rounds (in practice)
Max. barrel elevation/depression	+85°/–10°
Barrel elevation speed by hand	3° per turn
Rotation speed by hand	4° per turn
Rotated wt of whole	243kg
Wt of gun cradle	152.5kg
Wt of gun bed	71kg
Wt of chassis	2.162 tonnes
Wt of sights	87kg
Wt of electric motor	630kg
Total weight	3.67 tonnes

Note: All values for the 3.7cm Flak are provisional as precise information for a type cannot be established in the absence of the vintage (e.g. Flak 18, Flak 36 or 37). Individual weapons types varied one from another enormously in characteristics, not to mention the predictor gears. Calibre L/83 for the 1930 3.7cm Flak is very doubtful. The total length was always L/98; only for Flak 43 was the calibre length even close, at L89.2. The grooving was the same for all, 49.4 L/57. Flak 36 and 37 played the major role aboard German warships. Details common to both weapons are as follows: muzzle energy 22 megatonnes; muzzle velocity 820m/sec; disintegration range 3,500–6,600m; maximum range at 80° elevation 4,800m; weight of projectile 0.625kg; magazine weight 1.51kg; total weight of clip plus 6 rounds 12.5kg; rate of fire 160 rounds/min (in theory), 80–100 rounds (in practice).

2cm Flak

Description	2cm Flak /L65 C30 on centre-pivotal chassis C30
Calibre	20mm
Muzzle velocity (V_0)	835m/sec
Barrel length	65cal/1.3m
Length of bore	65cal/1.3m
Designed gas pressure	2,800kg/cm^2
Barrel life	22,000 rounds
Recoil energy	250kg
Length of grooving	72cm
Weight of barrel and breech	64kg
Maximum range	4,900m surface target, 3,700m ceiling
Wt of projectile	134g
Length of projectile	7.85cm
Wt of charge	39.5g
Total shell wt	320g
Overall length of shell	20.3cm
Rate of fire	280 rounds/min (in theory), 120 rounds/min in practice
Max. barrel elevation/depression	+85°/–11°
Wt of rotatable unit	43kg
Wt of chassis minus sights	282kg
Wt of gun	420kg

Details for the later 2cm quadruple Flak where varying from the above:

Description	2cm Flak /65 C38 on quadruple chassis C38
Rate of fire	1,800 rounds/min (in theory), 880 rounds (in practice)
Wt of rotatable unit	410kg
Wt of chassis minus sights	828kg
Wt of sights minus rotating gear	96.6kg
Wt of machinery	31.5kg
Wt of armour	500kg
Wt of complete gun	2.25 tonnes

Note: As with the 3.7cm Flak, there were substantial differences within the weapon type. The 2cm single Flak had a muzzle velocity of 900m/sec, a range of 4,800m (3,700m ceiling) and a disintegration lower height of 2,200m. Weights: cartridge 0.3kg; round 0.123kg; impact fuze/48 6.2g; magazine with 20 rounds 9.5kg. The gun had a theoretical rate of fire of 480 rounds/min (quadruple unit 1,800 rounds/min) but in practice the figure was 220 rounds/min (quadruple 720–800 rounds/min).

4cm Flak

This new Flak weapon – according to an unconfirmed source a German development discarded as unsatisfactory and marketed abroad – eventually saw service aboard Kriegsmarine units in the latter phases of the war as a replacement for the inadequate 3.7cm Flak.

Description	4cm Flak Bofors 28
Calibre	40mm
Muzzle velocity (V_0)	854m/sec
Barrel length	2.249m
Length of grooving	1.932m
Barrel life	10,000 rounds/barrel
Wt of projectile	0.955kg
Wt of charge	0.303kg
Maximum range	7,000m

GENERAL

It is interesting to examine the range of Flak weapons available to the Kriegsmarine and the operational effectiveness of the ammunition. The following is a comprehensive list of all Flak guns installed ashore and on board ship during the Second World War:

	Max. range (m)	Ceiling (m)	Disintegration ht (m)	Note
2cm MG C/30 C38	4,800	3,700	2,200	
3cm 103/38	5,730	2,600	1,600	1
3cm Mk 303	–	4,700	–	1
3.7cm SK C/30, C/30U, 36/37, Flak M42, M43	6,600	4,800	3,500	2
4cm Flak (Bofors)	9,600	6,700	c.5,000	3
5cm Flak 41	12,400	short 4,000	long 6,500	4
5.5cm Flak (Gerät 58/projected)	–	–	c.4,500	
7.5cm SK C34 multi-purpose	12,300	10,000	6,000+	5
8.8cm Flak SK C/31	17,800	13,300	10,600	6
8.8cm Flak SK C/32	17,200	12,400	10,600	6, 7
10.5cm Flak SK C/33	17,700	12,800	11,200	6
12.8cm Flak 40 (land-based only)	20,900	14,800	12,800	6

Notes
(1) Adapted from aircraft weapon for installation aboard E-boats and other small units.
(2) The frequently quoted range of 8,500m (ceiling 6,800m) relates to the SK C/30 V project only.
(3) Aboard ship only HE tracer was used operationally.
(4) Short = HE41 tracer, Long = HE41(8)
(5) Developed from the 7.5cm Flak L/60 (the so-called 'Versailles Flak'). From 1935 most of it was sold abroad, the remainder being used aboard German warships.
(6) Normally the fuze activated within the disintegration band when the tracer flare was extinguished. Here an independent fuze intervened.
(7) Gun used exclusively shipboard. With a rate of fire of 25 rounds/min in 1939, this gun was unmatched in the world.

Ammunition Stock: *Admiral Graf Spee* Commerce-Raiding Cruise, 1939

630–720 rounds 28cm
800–1000 rounds 15cm
2,400–3,000 rounds 10.5cm
8,000–24,000 rounds 3.7cm
24,000 rounds 2cm

SUMMARY

The ammunition for each individual Flak calibre was uniform throughout the Wehrmacht. Apparent differences in performance are attributable to barrel construction quality (very rarely) or to the various powered mountings and methods of stabilisation. A ship sailing alone might fire non-disintegrating ammunition, but to have actual projectiles rather than small metal splinters falling back into a friendly naval group was undesirable. The period of the tracer burn was linked to the fuze of the projectile, and the setting of the tracer determined the approximate altitude at which the shell burst. The method was only relatively accurate because of production factors (a point true for all navies). To be effective against low-flying aircraft at close range, the impact fuze was effective virtually instantaneously, but otherwise fuzes were set on a time, as opposed to a barometric, basis, the latter having too great a moment of inertia.

Whereas in a naval battle the object was to achieve a hit, the Flak aimed to shoot down or visibly damage an attacking aircraft as a secondary effect. Shell bursts and the puffs of smoke which accompanied them were intended to intimidate the aircraft crew and 'put them off', and so gunnery factors such as accuracy and speed of projectile ascent were – with few exceptions – relatively unimportant. The effective area was the approach height of the enemy at any particular moment in time. To penetrate the armour deck, every bomb had a release height corresponding to its weight. This height had been around 3,000m for years and gave a ship time to carry out an evasive manoeuvre after the bomb had been dropped. This changed towards the end of the war with the introduction of specialised designs and rocket-propelled bombs. Pure rocket-shells were fired in steep-angle attacks.

The increasing strength of bomber formations dictated a stronger defence; thus twin and quadruple mountings made their appearance in step with a larger shipboard Flak battery. Larger Flak calibres were introduced and armour was increased to counter the growing threat from dive-bombers.

Greater aircraft speeds and manoeuvrability presented serious problems for the light and medium weapons, slow to elevate and train laterally, which were also encumbered with impracticable shell hoists. The protection afforded Flak crews was inadequate and casualties were unnecessarily high.

The 12.8cm Flak twin (later with the addition of 'Euklid') was introduced aboard ship as the war progressed. The OKM required triaxial stabilisation to enable a uniform response to command transmissions. Including foundations and hoists but excluding armour, this would have resulted in a total weight of about 85 tonnes (the US 5in – 12.7cm – 38cal Mk 28/3 AA gun had a weight of 77 tonnes including armour). Even the 10.5cm Flak C/38 weighed 45 tonnes.

Taken as a whole, Flak was primarily a weapon of deterrence. A curtain of exploding HE projectiles was intended to unnerve aircraft crews and spoil their aim. It was less important to obtain a hit, which only became the priority when an aircraft penetrated into close proximity to the ship.

Below: *Deutschland* during her trials. The black, white and red merchant marine flag at the ensign staff shows that the ship is not yet in commission.

Fire Control and Radar

FIRE CONTROL AND RANGEFINDING EQUIPMENT

For main armament:

Foretop	1 × 10.5m rangefinder
Aft command centre	1 × 10.5m rangefinder
'A' turret	1 × 10.5m rangefinder
'B' turret	1 × 10.5m rangefinder

For medium armament:

Forward command centre	1 × 7m rangefinder

For Flak:

Flak control centre battle-mast* and astern	2 × 3m rangefinders
From 1935, both sides of battle-mast	2 × SL 2 in *Deutschland*; 2 × SL 4 in others
Aft command centre	1 × SL 4 (not *Deutschland*)

RADAR

Deutschland/Lützow

From 1937 *Deutschland* carried a Seetakt FuMG 39(go) installation, later converted to a FuMO 22. The demountable 0.8 × 1.8m aerial was fitted on the cupola of the foretop rangefinder and covered with a tarpaulin when not in use. The equipment was permanently replaced later by a FuMO 22 with 2 × 6m aerial. Bewteen January 1942 and March 1944 a FuMB 7 Timor aerial was located at the right side of the foretop radar centre.

Admiral Scheer

Fitted with a FuMO 22 ranging radar, initially replaced during the ship's major refit by a FuMO 27 (26?) with a 2 × 4m aerial. This was sited on the foretop rangefinder cupola, and a second FuMO 27 was installed later on the aft command centre rangefinder cupola. An FuMB 7 Timor was fitted at the foretop forward radar post and four FuMB 4 Sumatra dipole aerials were attached to platform extensions below the foretop rangefinder.

---

* Or, in Western parlance, the forward or bridge superstructure. The German terms are *Turmmast* ('tower mast'), *Gefechtsmast* ('battle mast') or *Gefechtsturm* ('battle tower').

Admiral Graf Spee

Fitted with an experimental FuMO 22 on the foretop rangefinder cupola.

Details

FuMO 22	Wavelength 81.5cm, frequency band 500kHz, initial output 8kW, range 14–18km, accuracy ±3°, frequency 368MHz.
FuMO 26	As above but range 20–25km, accuracy ±0.25°.

Below: *Deutschland*'s battle-mast from the port side. The pennant is that of a Konteradmiral (Rear-Admiral). At the foretop is the 10.5m rangefinder and, in descending order, are the main gunnery control centre, the foretop platform with its armoured surround, the main searchlight and then the Flak direction equipment. At the side, and a little lower, is a Type SL 2 Flak control system.

Machinery

DRIVE MACHINERY
Four sets geared drive motors each with two diesel motors turning two shafts.

Diesel type — Eight MAN 9-cylinder double-acting two-stroke motors Type M 9 Z 42/58 producing 6,655PSe = 6,563hp maximum endurance output each, 7,100PSe = 7,002hp maximum short-period output at 450 revs/min
Four auxiliary MAN 5-cylinder double-acting two stroke motors Type M 5 Z 42/58 producing 3,500PSe = 3,452hp maximum endurance output, 3,800PSe = 3,748hp maximum short-period performance at 425 revs/min

Contracts placed — *Deutschland* Oct. 1928; *Admiral Scheer* 17.7.31; *Admiral Graf Spee* 8.6.33

Motors — Average piston speed 8.7m/sec
Average effective pressure:
   Main motors 5.1kg/cm^2
   Auxiliary motors 5.2kg/cm^2
   Efficiency/litre 5.14PSe = 5.07hp/litre
Specific fuel consumption 200g/shp
Motor output/kg 11.52/PSe, 11.34kg/hp
Cylinder bore 420mm
Hub 580mm

Drive demands

Piston rods, cross-section I	*Deutschland, Scheer* 1,055kg/cm^2 *Graf Spee* 935kg/cm^2
Piston rods, cross-section II	*Deutschland, Scheer* 1,000kg/cm^2 *Graf Spee* 925kg/cm^2
Crosshead, cross-section I	*Deutschland* 500kg/cm^2 *Scheer* 545 (450) kg/cm^2 *Graf Spee* 490kg/cm^2
Crosshead, cross-section II	All 555kg/cm^2
Drive rods, cross-section I	All 530kg/cm^2
Drive rods, cross-section II	All 1,235kg/cm^2

All values quoted are at an ignition pressure of 55 at. The value in parentheses above for *Admiral Scheer* refers to the condition following the major refit.

Division of Motor Rooms
Housed in watertight compartments VI–XI.
Port side: Motor Room I – Drive Room I – Motor Room II.
Starboard side: Motor Room III – Drive Room II – Motor Room IV.

At 61.5m, the machinery rooms occupied 34% of the ships' length. Motor drive stations were situated in Motor Rooms I and III with sub-stations in Motor Rooms II and IV. The machinery control centre was situated on the upper platform deck port side. The motor output was transferred to the two shafts through a Vulcan reduction gear. In *Deutschland* four motors could be coupled to a single drive.

Aboard *Admiral Scheer* and *Admiral Graf Spee*, the drive was divided so that no more than two motors worked on any drive set. Auxiliary motors supplied the main motor fans, water coolant, oil coolant, lubricant and air pumps.

The maximum shaft speed was 250rpm. The shaft output for *Deutschland* was 27,000PSe = 26,629hp, the designed output per motor 6,750PSe = 6,750hp. The designed speed for *Deutschland* was 26kt at 54,000PSe = 53,259hp, but over the measured mile she achieved 28kt at only 48,390PSe = 47,726hp; *Admiral Scheer* managed 28.3kt at 52,050PSe = 51,336hp. The total output was 56,800PSe = 56,021hp, and after deduction of the drive loss 54,530PSe = 53,782hp.

Range (*Deutschland*)

1 motor per shaft	17,400nm, 13kt (19,700nm, 13kt anticipated)
2 motors per shaft	11,600nm, 19 kt
3 motors per shaft	7,900nm, 22kt
4 motors per shaft	4,750nm, 23.7kt

Motion was effected through two shafts each fitted with a three-bladed propeller (diameter *Deutschland* 3.97m, later 4.4m; *Admiral Scheer* and *Admiral Graf Spee* 3.82m).

The total performance weight, including fuel, water, auxiliary machinery, shafts, propellers and replacement parts, was 22.3kg/hp.

The total weight of all main and auxiliary machinery with fuel was 2,078.2 tonnes.

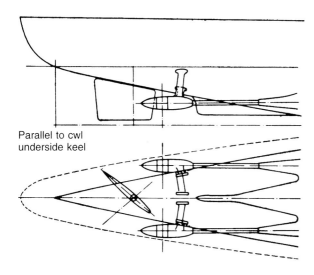

Parallel to cwl
underside keel

Above: Schematic representation of rudder and propeller arrangement.

Admiral Graf Spee: Fuel Consumption Trials

Trial	1	2
Speed (kt)	18.69	26.0
rpm	146	214
No of motors per shaft	2	4
No of auxiliary motors running	1	2
Output (PSe)	10,250	36,945
Fuel consumption, specific (g/PSh)	248	226
Consumption, E-diesel motors (kg/h)	160	160
Consumption, auxiliary boilers (kg/h)	415	415
Total consumption (tonnes/h)	3,117	8,925
Ship's range based on figures (nm)	16,300	7,900
Consumption per 100nm (tonnes)	16.8	34.2

Stopping Trials

From speed (kt)	Stopping distance (m)	Stopping time	Stopping distance, all engines full astern (m)	Stopping time, all engines full full astern
9	1,190	8min 49sec	394	2min 38sec
13	1,710	9min	720	2min 40sec
17	2,215	8min 38sec	740	2min 35sec
21	2,420	9min 20sec	840	2min 22sec
26	3,000	9min 30sec	780	2min 20sec

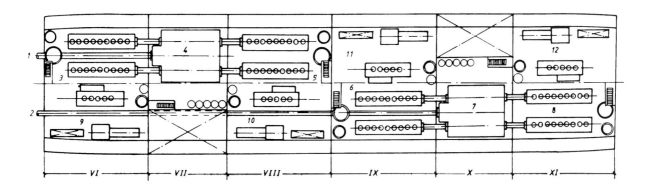

Above: Schematic representation of engine room plant aboard *Deutschland* (arrangement of drive machinery in *Admiral Scheer* and *Admiral Graf Spee* differed): (1) Port shaft. (2) Starboard shaft. (3) Motor Room I (port) Compartment VI. (4) Drive Room I (port) Compartment VII. (5) Motor Room II (port) Compartment VIII. (6) Motor Room III (starboard) Compartment IX. (7) Drive Room II (starboard) Compartment X. (8) Motor Room IV (starboard) Compartment XI. (9) Electrical Plant I (starboard) Compartment VI. (10) Electrical Plant II (starboard) Compartment VIII. (11) Electrical Plant III (port) Compartment X. (12) Electrical Plant IV (port) Compartment XI.

Mileage Trials

No of motors in operation	Shaft output (shp)	Speed (kt)	rpm	Draught fwd (m)	Draught aft (m)
2	358	5.38	45	5.8	7.27
2	1,659	10.06	79	5.8	7.27
2	3,775	13.52	105	5.9	7.24
2	4,590	14.69	114	5.8	7.23
4	9,770	18.34	142	5.8	7.27
4	15,130	20.68	164	5.9	7.24
4	19,125	22.22	176	5.9	7.24
6	24,675	23.5	190	5.8	7.23
6	31,015	24.87	204	5.8	7.23
8	36,125	26.0	213	5.8	7.27
8	53,650	28.5	240	5.8	7.27

Electric Motor Installation

There were four electric motor rooms (E-Werke) distributed between Compartments VI and XI in the main motor rooms as follows: EW-I (Stbd Compartment VI), EW-II (Stbd Compartment VIII), EWIII (Port Compartment IX) and EW-IV (Port Compartment XI). In each EW there were two diesel generators covering the needed demand of current, as follows:

Deutschland: 2,160kW
Admiral Scheer: 2,800kW
Admiral Graf Spee: 3,360kW. For this ship the Wilhelmshaven Navy Yard manufactured (probably under licence) an additional auxiliary unit as an electro-diesel installed in Motor Room IV.

Deutschland had 6-cylinder diesels with direct injection manufactured by Linke-Hoffmann-Busch of Breslau. These had an output of 375–440hp each and drove the 250kW AEG generators.

The units aboard *Admiral Scheer* were supplied by MAN and, at least initially, some of those in *Admiral Graf Spee* came from MWM. The following is valid for *Admiral Graf Spee* (and probably *Admiral Scheer*, but with differences for *Deutschland/Lützow*). Each of the four *E-Werke* had two diesel generators (total output 3,360kW, 220V DC). The switching centre was slung above it, below the armoured deck. The aggregates were situated in the respective motor rooms.

The 640 hp diesels were four-stroke machines with freshwater coolant itself re-cooled with seawater. The motors were started from the motor room; the generators switched into the main user circuit which could be divided port and starboard in the event of an emergency. Generator loadings were supervised by an ammeter (full loading 1,885 amps). There was no emergency aggregate (the additional auxiliary diesel built for *Admiral Graf Spee* at Wilhelmshaven apparently had some other function).

Horizontal Siemens transformers of 25kVA and 15kVA, 60V 50Hertz, were located in the switching centres. This AC supply served all engine room command relay centres and damage control. The major users of current were the ship's armament, the anti-roll system and the damage control pumps, of which last there were twelve, distributed throughout the watertight compartments, each with a demand capacity of 600m³/hr. An additional 24V DC transformer powered the shipboard telephone system, with a small accumulator battery as an emergency reserve.

Auxiliary Machinery

Each ship carried two auxiliary boilers located above the armoured deck and used to supply the galleys and fire pumps. *Admiral Scheer* and *Admiral Graf Spee* both had an anti-roll device fitted which proved unsatisfactory and was removed from the former ship during her 1940 refit, the space being converted into additional bunkers. Each motor room was equipped with a main fire pump.

Rudder Assembly

The rudder of each ship had a surface area of 49m² and was served by one or other independent motors, supported if necessary by a manual station located in the lower platform deck between Frames 22.25 and 26.5.

Helms

Main	Command bridge
Battle	Forward command centre
Reserves	Command control room and rudder motor room forward
Manual	Manual operation room

Anchor Installation

On completion each ship had one stern and three bow anchors. During later refits *Deutschland* and *Admiral Scheer* had one bow anchor unshipped.
Anchor type: Hall, weight 6,000kg, diameter of chain link 63mm, pull stress of chain 56.11 tonnes, weight of anchor chain 2.14 tonnes. On overseas voyages or in foreign waters

an 800kg Hall anchor was carried for warping. The stern anchor was only a third to half the weight of the bow anchor and had no chain, being attached to a very thick steel hawser also used for towing purposes. The bow anchor chains were measured in 25m lengths, the total length being nine lengths plus three in reserve stowed on the port side. A red/white mark at each 25m enabled the length of chain let out to be estimated.

Anti-Roll Installation
Following the early Atlantic voyage of *Deutschland* it was decided to install anti-roll gear which was in vogue at the time, and both *Admiral Scheer* and *Admiral Graf Spee* were duly fitted with it. The devices failed to meet expectations and did not improve sea-keeping. That aboard *Admiral Scheer* was landed during the 1940 refit, the space being converted to bunkers, but plans to remove *Admiral*

Graf Spee's unit were frustrated by the situation just prior to the outbreak of war.

The 7m wide steering gear for the installation was located amidships above the armoured deck at Frames 109 to 113.5. It comprised a control gyro, electric motor and supercharger. The control worked on a large tank with bottom flooding slots and was situated in the outer wall passages between Frames 98 to 122 on either side of the ship. The installation was only switched on when the ship was rolling and when the guns were in use. The supercharger used over 3,000 amps when running and a entire electric motor was needed to supply the operating current. One E-motor = two aggregates = a quarter of the ship's total machinery output. When the ship pitched, the device switched off automatically, and when the ship rolled it switched on automatically. This confused the gyroscope and rendered the installation ineffective.

Below: One of the eight welded-steel Type MAN M9 Zu 42/58 drive motors. Of light construction, they were double action, 9-cylinder, two-stroke diesels with a cylinder diameter of 420mm and a piston stroke of 520mm. Their output at 450 revolutions was 7,100hp. This diesel installation was the most powerful of its kind at the time.

Refits

Experiences obtained during the prewar oceanic voyages, such as the South Atlantic cruise by *Deutschland*, the gunnery trials in the western Atlantic and operations in Spanish waters, suggested the need for limited modifications to the ships. Beyond the relatively short chop of the North Sea and Baltic, the Panzerschiffe proved to be very wet forward, and at high speeds the stern tended to dig in, leaving the quarterdeck constantly awash. Topweight was another problem, particularly in *Admiral Scheer* and *Admiral Graf Spee* with their pagoda-like battle-masts. Suggestions for the reduction of the secondary armament by four gunhouses, the straight exchange of the secondary armament for twin 12.7cm multi-purpose weapons and doing away with the shipboard aircraft installation were rejected and eventually the idea of rebuilding the foreship of the two later units and replacing the existing battle-mast with a tubular mast similar to that aboard *Deutschland* came into favour. The raising of the lateral bulges to upper deck level to improve the side armour was planned, together with other modifications such as installing radar, improving the ship's wireless system, adding shipboard aircraft, stabilising the searchlights, supplying splinter shields for the small-calibre weapons and strengthening the foundations for the motors. These modifications would in total have amounted to little more than 70 tons extra weight per ship.

Further studies envisaged widening the beam, which would have resulted in a weight increase of 200 tons and a reduction in speed; a more acceptable variation was a broader beam, with greater length, which would have endowed the ships with greater speed but have prejudiced sea-keeping qualities, for a weight increase of 750 tons. Although this conversion, including improved splinter protection and engine room alterations, needed time, Admiral Raeder spoke out in its favour in 1938 when the first decisions in this direction were finally announced, twelve-month refits being scheduled for *Admiral Scheer* (from January 1940), *Admiral Graf Spee* (from June 1942) and *Deutschland* (from December 1942).

A memorandum entitled 'Sea War Policy against Britain', a treatise concerning German naval building plans from autumn 1938, remarked in respect of the *Deutschland* class: 'The first Panzerschiffe are such a valuable type of ship that an improvement in speed (to 28–30kt) would bring rewards. Even if with the speed increase they fail to match results obtained in cruiser warfare by the new Panzerschiffe (i.e. *Scharnhorst* and *Gneisenau*), there are certain valuable complementary tasks which they can undertake. In oceanic cruiser warfare, with a top speed at present of 25kt, their life expectancy is short.' The outbreak of war in 1939 and the periods of international tension preceding it put an end to these plans. *Deutschland* and *Admiral Scheer* were indeed ultimately rebuilt, but not in the manner envisaged prewar.

A large percentage of all refit work involved the ship's machinery, and this always provoked a fresh outbreak of virulent criticism directed at the diesel engines. It is true that there were difficulties initially. But to lay blame on the manufacturer was as reprehensible as to pretend that the engines were perfect. In Works Circular No 5012 entitled 'Rumours about MAN Diesel Installations aboard the German Panzerschiffe', issued at Augsburg on 24 January 1935, the company drew attention to the fact that 'the shipbuilding press, especially overseas, has recently referred to a number of reports that our diesel motors have proved unsatisfactory. These reports, which apparently originate from certain interested circles, quote excessive engine vibration and noise and argue for a return to steam turbines for new warships . . . we are aware that certain rumours are being deliberately circulated . . . we cannot ask the Navy for their feelings in the matter but confirm that MAN diesels give great satisfaction now as before . . .'

These negative reports undoubtedly influenced the decision of the Kriegsmarine to revert to steam turbine propulsion when the question next arose following completion of the three Panzerschiffe. The medium/fast-running MAN large-ship diesels were naturally not without their faults, and these were not fully ironed out until 1941. But the advantage of having them outweighed everything because they were the ideal machinery for oceanic commerce raiders.

In the Kriegsmarine circles which mattered, the boiler and turbine manufacturers had numerous lobbyists whereas MAN's only representative, Pielstik, the Senior

Engineer, could not afford to waste days on end in naval chambers 'waiting to be seen'. It was 1938 before the Kriegsmarine suddenly realised the pressing need for the development of new diesels for the new Z-Plan battleships, but by then they had missed the bus. Bearing in mind the contractural precondition imposed by the Reichsmarine that MAN must supply the lightest engines possible, this being ultimately the real reason underlying the later defects, the observations of a MAN specialist involved in the work on the *Deutschland* are enlightening: 'I would like to make the point here that MAN engineers made every possible effort to reduce the engine unit weight per hp . . . In the end this [the precondition] was not clever at all, for the ship rode too high in the water, and she had to be ballasted with . . . cast iron ribs. The designers would have found this enormous extra weight very useful for producing a stronger and more solid engine structure . . .' No further comment is necessary.

Basic Structural Differences between the Ships of the Class

The battle-mast on *Deutschland* was tubular; *Admiral Graf Spee* and *Admiral Scheer* had pagoda-like battle-masts (on the latter ship this was replaced by a tubular mast in 1940). The aircraft catapult aboard *Deutschland* was installed between the battle-mast and funnel, but on the other two ships it was sited abaft the funnel. The pole mast mounted to the rear of the funnel reached down to the superstructure deck on *Admiral Graf Spee* but only to the platform deck on *Admiral Scheer*.

Refits and Modifications

1935

Deutschland: A shipboard aircraft catapult was mounted between battle-mast and funnel. Two He 60 floatplanes were shipped, one being a reserve in its component parts. A 'landing sail' was fitted on the port side. The port loading derrick was replaced by a lattice crane. Three 8.8cm Flak singles were replaced by twin mountings of the same calibre. The fire control installations were modernised. The battle-mast was enlarged by the addition of a foretop gallery. The calibre of the torpedo tube sets was increased from 50cm to 53.3cm. New aerial outriggers, and between them a pole mast, were mounted on the rear of the funnel cap. A new dome was fitted to the rangefinder of the aft control centre.

Admiral Scheer: An aircraft catapult was installed abaft the funnel. A retrieval crane for the aircraft was mounted on the starboard side but removed later that year. A 'landing sail' was fitted portside.

1936

Admiral Scheer: Pressure bulkheads were fitted forward and aft of the 15cm guns.

1937

Deutschland: Pressure bulkheads were fitted forward and aft of the 15cm guns. The lattice crane and starboard derrick were unshipped and replaced by different crane types. Noise suppressors were fitted inside the funnel and a searchlight platform was mounted on derrick posts at the funnel sides. A radar aerial was installed in the foretop sometime in the autumn.

Admiral Scheer: The armorial shield at the stem was redesigned.

1938

Deutschland: The funnel received a slightly raked cap.

Admiral Scheer: An ensign gaff was mounted at the rear of the foretop but later shifted to the rear of the foretop radar dome. The battle-mast received additional platforms, including an admiral's bridge with extensions. The yards of the mainmast abaft the funnel were shortened and the ends gaffed.

Admiral Graf Spee: The six 8.8cm twin Flak guns were replaced by six 10.5cm on the same mountings. A mattress aerial for the FMG G(gO) (= FuMO 22) radar was installed on the foretop rangefinder. The corners of the octagonal foretop were rounded. The battle-mast was rebuilt. The two searchlights at the sides of the funnel were replaced by a single forward-facing searchlight on a platform at the same height.

1939

Deutschland was given a FuMO 22 radar aerial at the foretop. The floatplane 'landing sail' was landed and the He 60 biplanes replaced by the new Ar 196.

Admiral Scheer: The straight-armed crane portside was replaced by a crane of different design. The 'landing sail' was landed and the He 60 exchanged for Ar 196. On the foretop rotating dome a radar position minus aerial was installed for a FuMO 22 set.

Admiral Graf Spee: The 'landing sail' was jettisoned in the South Atlantic.

1940

Deutschland was rebuilt, the straight stem and a number of frames making way for a slight clipper bow; the hull was

1.9m longer as a result. One of the two portside anchors was unshipped and a degaussing system was installed. The 8.8cm twin Flak guns were replaced by six 10.5cm L/65 C/33 heavy twin Flaks in C31 mountings. The light Flak was augmented to four 3.7cm twins and numerous 2cm.

Admiral Scheer: In a major refit, the pagoda-like battle-mast was replaced by a tubular mast, the stem was replaced and the hull lengthened as in *Deutschland*. A tripod mainmast was erected abaft the funnel and a new crane installed portside. The anti-roll system was unshipped. The 8.8cm twin Flak were replaced by 10.5cm twin mountings. The funnel received a slightly raked cap. A degaussing system was fitted. An FuMO 27 radar aerial was mounted on the foretop cupola and the FuMO 22 equipment installed in 1939 was exchanged. The light Flak was increased and the ship's machinery was overhauled.

1941

Admiral Scheer: A FuMO 26 radar with aerial was installed at the aft command centre.

1942

Deutschland: A FuMB 4 radar was installed at the rear of the foretop and a FuMO 26 radar with two aerials replaced the FuMO 22. The funnel received a raked cap.

Admiral Scheer: Four Sumatra sets were installed on the foretop coaming forward and sides and a Timor set on the rear face of the radar dome. The funnel received a raked cap. The projecting foretop platform was unshipped and searchlights on the funnel platform were reduced by one to three. In the foretop, the FuMO 22 equipment installed in 1941 was replaced by FuMO 26 with two aerials.

1943

Admiral Scheer: The two FuMO 26 aerials were replaced by a single aerial.

1944

Deutschland: The two FuMO 26 aerials were replaced by a single aerial. The Flak armament now comprised six 4cm Bofors 28, four 3.7cm (aft) and 26 2cm (three quadruples and six twins with splinter shields and two unshielded singles).

1945

Deutschland: The Flak armament was increased to ten 3.7cm and 28 2cm.

Admiral Scheer: the Flak armament was increased to six 4cm Bofors 28, eight 3.7cm and 33 2cm.

Below: German warship ensigns: top left, the North German Federation, later Bismarck's Second Reich, from 1 October 1867; top right, the black, white and red tricolour of the Reichsmarine from 1 January 1922, bearing in the canton the colours of the Weimar Republic; bottom left, the tricolour with the canton removed as of 16 March 1933; and bottom right, the Reich War Flag introduced on 7 November 1935.

Scale Plans

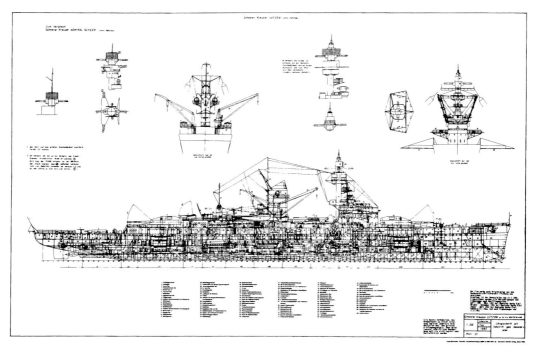

Above: Longitudinal section, with masts and rigging.
Below: 'Tween deck, armoured deck and upper platform deck per general plan.

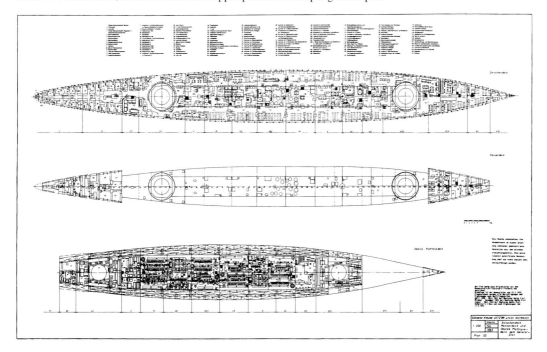

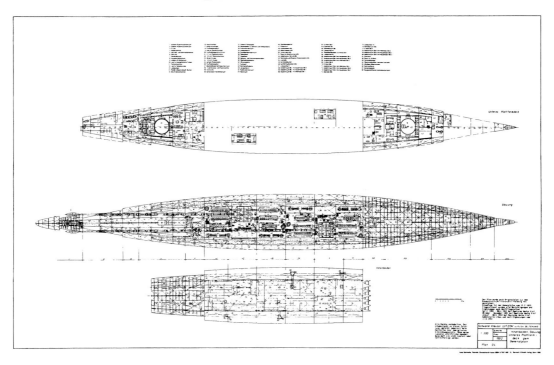

Above: Inner bottom, plant room and lower platform deck.
Below: Cross-sections per general plan.

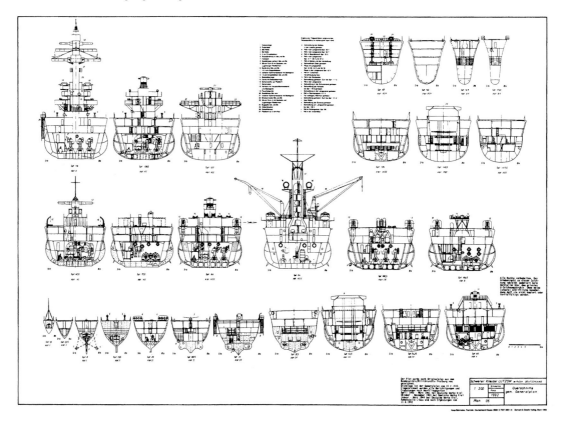

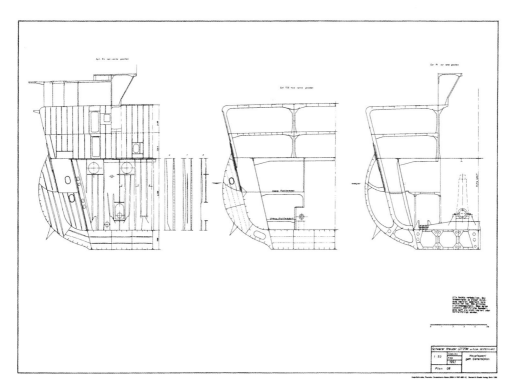

Above: Main frame per general plan.
Below: Frame plan.

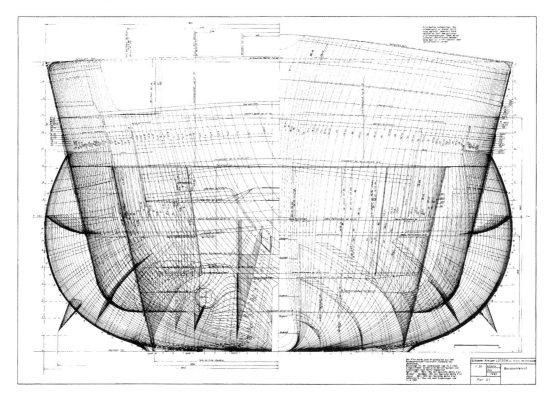

41

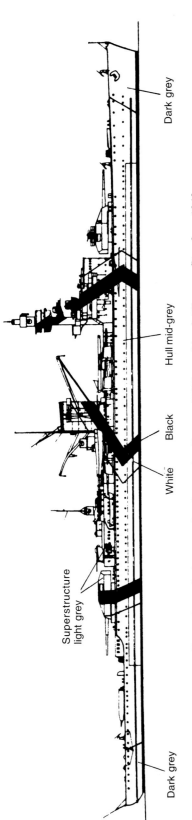

Superstructure
light grey

White

Black

Hull mid-grey

Dark grey

Dark grey

Camouflage scheme for heavy cruiser *Lützow* (ex *Panzerschiff Deutschland*). Weapons fit as from 1943.

Lützow: camouflage scheme, port side, Norway, 1942.

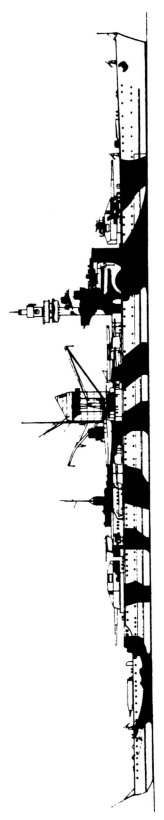

Lützow: camouflage scheme, starboard side, Norway, 1942.

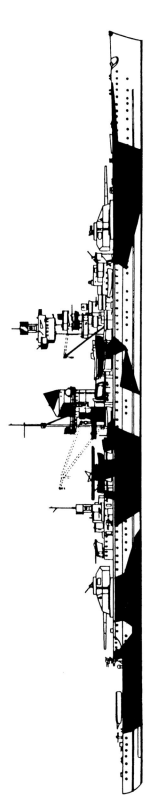

Admiral Scheer: camouflage scheme, Norway, 1942 (port and starboard sides similar).

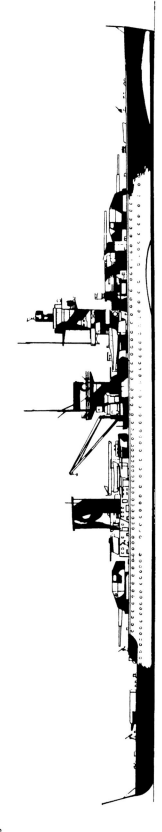

Admiral Graf Spee, showing the disguise adopted during her anti-shipping cruise, 1939: the dummy wood-and-canvas second funnel, from which thick smoke would be emitted on sighting enemy vessels; and the dummy wooden superfiring main turret forward and other temporary fittings on the bridge superstructure. The false bow waves were intended to confuse observers as to the ship's true speed.

Panzerschiff *Deutschland*

The building contract for the ship was placed with the Deutsche Werke Yard, Kiel, as Panzerschiff 'A' (= 'Replacement *Preussen*'), Builder's Number 219. The keel was laid on 5 February 1929, the hull being launched on 19 May 1931. An estimated 60,000 spectators attended. All naval vessels in the harbour fired a 21-gun salute on the arrival of Reich President von Hindenburg.

Reich Chancellor Dr Brüning delivered the baptismal speech, and the naming ceremony was intended to be performed by Hindenburg. However, at this stage too great a number of stoppers at the seaward end of the slip were removed prior to the launch by shipyard staff and the hull set off as Hindenburg was preparing to deliver his address, tearing away the cable network for the microphones.

The first tug-assisted floating trials, mainly for engine testing, were carried out on 5 November 1932. Full trials were carried out the following year, on 18 and 19 January and 8 February, after which the ship transferred to Wilhelmshaven for completion on 27/28 February. Successful acceptance trials were run off Heligoland on 27 February 1933 and the ship was commissioned on 1 April by Kapitän zur See Hermann von Fischel. Shortly before the ceremony, 474 men embarked en masse from the refitting light cruiser *Emden*. This brought the peacetime complement to its full strength of 643 officers, men and civilians (33 officers, 24 warrant officers, ten senior NCOs, 121 junior NCOs, 440 lower rates plus fifteen civilians, the last consisting of eight cooks and stewards, one barber, three shoemakers and three tailors).

In mid-May 1933 *Deutschland* took about 100 MAN diesel engineers aboard for her maiden commissioning voyage from Wilhelmshaven via the Skagerrak to Kiel, where she was present on the 22nd of the month for a Fleet Review attended by the Reich Chancellor. Hitler raised his standard on the Fleet flagship *Schleswig-Holstein* and later the light cruiser *Leipzig* while observing the naval exercises, but *Deutschland* remained at her moorings at Kiel and took no part, resuming her maiden voyage upon their conclusion. She visited Balholmen in Norway and the Faroes, passed by way of the Denmark Strait to Iceland and, after a short ceremony of commemoration in the Skagerrak for the German dead of the Battle of Jutland, berthed at Wilhelmshaven on 1 June.

The engine trials had proved very satisfactory. It was found that a speed of 25kt could be maintained at 377rpm; the ship had run six to ten hours at 390rpm, three to five hours at 400rpm and an hour at maximum output (about 28kt). These statistics showed that her range was 11,600 nautical miles at 19kt.

Ventilation channels were re-routed and noise suppressors fitted to the exhaust piping as a result of excessive fumes in the motor rooms and intolerable noise levels respectively. Flying sparks were given off at above 390rpm, which twice resulted in funnel fires, and fire watchers were stationed on the funnel platform whenever the ship's speed exceeded 21kt.

On 6 June Deutschland re-entered the Baltic and in deep water off Pillau recorded a speed of 28.2kt over the measured mile. Gunnery trials in company with the target ship *Baden* commenced on 30 June. Initially practice rounds were used, followed by Abkommschiessen, in which the heavy and medium armament were exercised firing smaller-calibre ammunition through a specially fitted barrel lining. The exercises culminated with the use of live shells at night. On 10 December *Deutschland* completed her period of trials and was assigned to the BdL (Befehlshaber der Linienschiffe, or C-in-C Battleships).

1934

During the first few months of the year *Deutschland* exercised and worked up. In April she sailed from Kiel for an unpublicised visit to the Norwegian fjords at Sogne and Hardanger. The Reich Chancellor embarked, together with high Party functionaries and military chiefs of staff. During his stay on board, Hitler made a substantial impression, conducting himself in the unassuming manner of a passenger, giving orders that he neither wished to be accorded special consideration on account of his position nor receive reports. Frequently he wandered alone through the ship and conversed with crew members.

After participating in the May naval exercises off Warnemünde and Sassnitz, *Deutschland* left Wilhelmshaven on 9 June in company with the light cruiser *Köln* for gunnery exercises in the Western Atlantic, calling in at Funchal and returning to Germany on 23 June.

In August the Swedish port of Göteborg was visited during the autumn naval exercises, and on 1 October *Deutschland* relieved *Schlesien* as the BdL flagship. After a call at Leith in Scotland, the ship docked at Wilhelmshaven for a refit beginning on 13 December.

1935

Deutschland left the yards on 21 February. On 14 March the BdL hoisted his pennant and the Panzerschiff sailed for Brazil, Trinidad and Aruba, principally for engine trials. Sea-keeping was found to be generally good, in heavy weather the major defects being flooding of the motor rooms through ventilation shafts and the forecastle shipping seas as far aft as the superstructure deck. These faults were later partially alleviated by the fitting of a breakwater forward of 'A' turret together with water deflectors to avert possible flooding of the shell platforms. *Deutschland* returned to Germany on 19 April, having spent 32 days at sea and covering 12,286nm at an average speed of 16kt. The ship's range with various motor combinations was found to be:

Motors per shaft	Speed (kt)	Range (nm)
One	13	17,400
Two	19	11,600
Three	22	7,900
Four	23.7	4,750

The ship's peacetime complement was increased to 33 officers and 943 men (including fourteen civilians), plus, for the first time, eleven Luftwaffe (naval air arm) servicemen. The ship took part in the routine August fleet gunnery exercises during which Hitler, von Blomberg, Raeder and Göring came aboard as observers, the last out of interest for the new shipboard aircraft installation. The catapult had been tested extensively ashore since 1932 but was prohibited aboard German ships by the Versailles Treaty and did not make its first appearance aboard Fleet units until after the declaration of military sovereignty by Hitler on 16 March (as retroactively sanctioned by the Anglo-German Naval Treaty of 18 June 1936). Aboard *Deutschland* the catapult was positioned between the battle-mast and funnel. A compressed air charge of 60 atmospheres was used to dispatch the He 60 floatplane. Ships were provided with a 'landing sail', a large mat towed

from a boom extended alongside the hull, the purpose of which was to support the aircraft on landing in the sea, but the idea proved of little value and the mats were gradually withdrawn.

Kapitän zur See Paul Fanger was appointed the second commander of *Deutschland* during September 1935. On 20 October the ship proceeded in company with *Admiral Scheer* to the Canaries and Azores for gunnery, range-finding and towing exercises. The swastika battle flag was ceremonially hoisted aboard ship for the first time on 7 November and *Deutschland* docked for a scheduled engine overhaul two days later. At this time work was also carried out on anti-aircraft and torpedo fittings.

1936

Crew training and exercises occupied the first half of the year. Between 29 and 31 May *Deutschland* was present at Kiel with the major part of the Fleet for the dedication by Hitler of the new naval monument at Laboe. Between 6 and 19 June the ship cruised by the north-about route to Copenhagen via Biscay and the Irish Sea, experiencing rolls of up to 40 degrees during heavy weather. In July gunnery and torpedo trials were run in the Baltic, interspersed with visits to seaside resorts to 'show the flag'. The Spanish Civil War broke out on 18 July, and on the

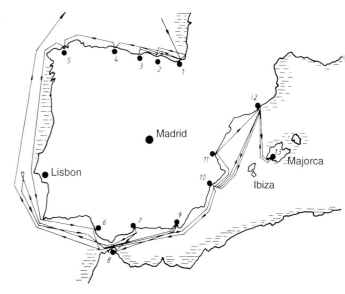

Above: Courses sailed and ports visited by *Deutschland* during the Spanish operation, 1936.
Key: (1) San Sebastian. (2) Bilbao. (3) Santander. (4) Gijon. (5) Corunna. (6) Cadiz. (7) Malaga. (8) Ceuta. (9) Almeria. (10) Alicante. (11) Valencia. (12) Barcelona. (13) Palma.

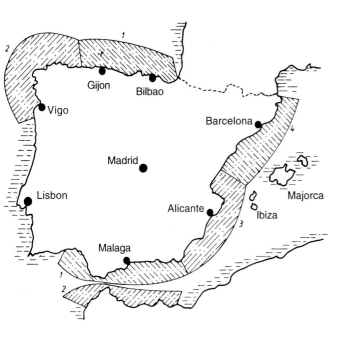

Above: The control zones laid down by the Non-Intervention Committee in London for the naval supervision of Spanish coastal waters.
Key: (1) British. (2) French. (3) German. (4) Italian.

23rd of the month *Deutschland*, together with other units exercising off Heligoland, was recalled to Wilhelmshaven. She made fast in the 'Alaska' anchorage, where live ammunition was shipped. The following day a formation consisting of the sister-ships *Deutschland* and *Admiral Scheer*, followed a little later by the light cruiser *Köln* and the 2nd Torpedo-boat Flotilla (these being the only serviceable large warships available) set off for Spanish waters under the command of the BdL, Vizeadmiral Carls. *Deutschland* anchored briefly at San Sebastian on the 26th, but eventually found it more comfortable in the heavy swell to cruise up and down at a few knots offshore. The German presence was purely humanitarian. Communication was maintained with Republican and Nationalist harbours without discrimination and refugees taken aboard were passed foward to one of the 26 merchant vessels chartered for evacuation purposes. The international operation involved the use of 62 such transports. About 9,300 refugees, including 4,550 Germans, were brought to safety.

By the end of July *Deutschland* had worked round to Corunna with calls at Bilbao and Gijon. An increasing danger had been perceived in these waters and the secondary armament and anti-aircraft crews remained on permanent alert. For recognition purposes the two main turrets were painted with black, white and red stripes, the national colours of Germany. In the first week of August, in company with one or both of the torpedo-boats *Luchs* and *Leopard*, stops were made at Cadiz, Almeria, Ceuta and Malaga. Tension was heightened when the Republican side declared all Nationalist harbours to be a war zone, and German warships avoided them initially. On 9 August *Deutschland* berthed at Barcelona two days before the Catalonian capital seceded from Spain and declared autonomy. The first Spanish voyage terminated at Wilhelmshaven on the 30th of the month.

On 3 August the French Government proposed the setting up of an international Non-Intervention Commission in which the warships of four nations (Britain, France, Germany and Italy) would maintain a general control of allotted sectors of the Spanish coast. The first meeting of the Commission was held on 9 September, but on 24 August the four powers had already signed an agreement to come into effect in 1937. The Kriegsmarine accepted responsibility for the Mediterranean coast between Cabo de Gata (Almeria) and Oropesa. Some of the signatory states followed the recommendations of the treaty only half-heartedly. Whereas the original intention of the German naval presence had been the protection of German lives and property, aggression by the Republican side had tended to identify them as the 'enemy'. In time, therefore, it would become apparent who was supporting whom.

Deutschland left Wilhelmshaven on 1 October for her second tour of duty off Spain and returned on 21 November, having patrolled the Bay of Alicante area. Normal peacetime naval exercises were cancelled as available German warships operated a system of alternating reliefs. As at mid-October, German naval forces had evacuated 15,397 people (including 5,539 Germans).

1937

On 31 January *Deutschland* left Kiel and on 6 February relieved *Admiral Graf Spee* off Cape Negro. Severe icing was encountered in winter storms on the way. The ship docked at Wilhelmshaven for a refit on 31 March. The two searchlight masts were replaced by a platform for four searchlights on the funnel; radio aerial outriggers were installed at the rear of the funnel cap; the former bar-type shipboard crane on the port side and the derrick to starboard amidships were removed in favour of cranes of more modern design; and so-called 'pressure bulkheads' were installed, improving the protection for the 15cm gun crews.

On 31 March, off Valencia, a Republican destroyer made a threatening torpedo-type approach to *Admiral Scheer*. In May warships of the four international control powers and the United States exercised jointly for the first time. *Deutschland* left Germany on 10 May and moored in the anchorage at Palma, Majorca, on the 24th, where Republican aircraft attacked the town and harbour installations that morning. *Deutschland*, the torpedo-boat *Albatros*, two U-boats and six Italian units were grouped together in the port and received attention, four bombs falling wide within 200yds. The Panzerschiff therefore moved to Ibiza, arriving there at 1815 hrs on 29th May. At 1840 hrs the alarm was raised when four Republican destroyers and two light cruisers, *Libertad* and *Mendez-Nuñez*, were seen approaching, and immediately afterwards two aircraft were reported 2km astern, attacking out of the sun at an altitude of 1,000m. Two 50kg bombs struck *Deutschland* while the destroyers, initially closing the German Panzerschiff as if to torpedo, opened an inaccurate fire with their forward armament, the shells falling short. The first bomb hit the roof of Starboard III 15cm gunhouse, splinters puncturing the fuel tank of the floatplane on the catapult. The leaking aviation spirit caught fire in the area of the Senior NCOs' mess. A motor launch and the aircraft were destroyed. The second bomb had a devastating effect, penetrating as far as the 'tween deck at Frame 116, the ensuing explosion and fire destroying the upper deck between Frames 94 and 145. A jet of flame ignited oil and spirits beyond an open bulkhead door at Frame 121 and this fire spread rapidly. The forward 15cm magazine was flooded immediately as a precaution. The worst of the casualties occurred to the personnel of 'A' turret, and it was twenty minutes before these guns could be trained on the approaching Republican destroyers, which ceased fire and turned away when ready ammunition for the 15cm starboard battery exploded at 1930. At the time of the disaster no special state of alert was in effect aboard *Deutschland* and the AA guns were probably not manned – a grave omission after the warning in Majorca a few days previously.

By 1935 the situation was under control, allowing *Deutschland* to weigh anchor and sail for a rendezvous with *Admiral Scheer* off Formentera. The final casualty list was 31 dead and 110 wounded, 71 seriously, these being mostly burn cases. As a reprisal for the attack, on 31 May *Admiral Scheer* bombarded the harbour at Almeria. Meanwhile *Deutschland* had landed 35 seriously wounded at Gibraltar on 30 May, a further 34 wounded being put ashore the next day when the ship was ordered to sea. The British authorities arranged a military funeral for the

dead in the late afternoon of 1 June, but on Hitler's order the bodies were exhumed on the 11th, the coffins being brought alongside *Deutschland* by lighter and placed under 'B' turret with an honour guard. The bodies of three casualties interred at Ibiza arrived aboard *Leopard* on 9 June.

During the homeward voyage no effort was spared in repairing or camouflaging the damage. *Deutschland* berthed at Wilhelmshaven in the evening of 15 June ,when

Below: The air attack on *Deutschland*, 29 May 1937.
Key: (1) *Deutschland*'s anchorage. (2) Bombing run out of the sun and escape route of attacking aircraft. (3) Fall of shell fired by approaching Republican destroyers.

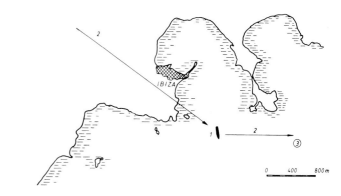

Below: After the attack.

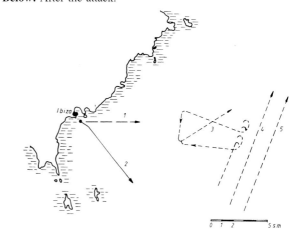

Key: (1) Escape route of attacking aircraft. (2) Course of *Deutschland* after weighing anchor. (3) Course of attacking Republican destroyers. (4) Course of Republican cruisers *Libertad* and *Mendez-Nuñez*. (5) Course of cruisers' destroyer escort.

the commander and BdL addressed the crew before the coffins were conveyed by lorry in a torchlit procession through crowded streets to the military cemetery. The mass burial was held on 17 June before many thousand onlookers, Hitler being present with a large entourage.

Repairs to *Deutschland* took ten days, after which the ship took part in restricted naval exercises. Kapitän zur See Paul Wenneker became the ship's third commander, and on 5 October the cruiser returned to Spanish waters and visited El Ferrol, Cadiz, Tangier, Algeciras, Ceuta and Melilla. By then Germany had withdrawn from the international control following two submarine attacks on the light cruiser *Leipzig* off the Algerian port of Oran on 15 and 18 June. *Deutschland* called at the Italian port of Gaeta on 14 November and spent the Christmas and New Year period at Naples, with short excursions to Capri, Amalfi and Taormina accompanied by destroyers and torpedo-boats.

1938

Deutschland arrived at Wilhelmshaven on 11 February as flagship of the BdP (Befehlshaber der Panzerschiffe, or C-in-C Panzerschiffe), Vizeadmiral von Fischel, her former commander, having embarked at El Ferrol. In drydock strengthening repairs were carried out on structural defects to the foundations to Motor Rooms I and IV. Between 24 July and 15 August the ship voyaged to Tangier and Gibraltar. On 22 August she was at Kiel for the last great German Naval Review in the presence of Hitler, to mark the launch of the heavy cruiser *Prinz Eugen*. When *Deutschland* left Kiel for the Atlantic at the time of the Sudeten Crisis on 20 September, she embarked a 'mobilisation supplement' of weapons and other technical officers and prize captains together with tropical clothing. Since the autumn of 1937 she had carried a radar aerial in the foretop which was removed in harbour, but during her stay at Vigo between 22 and 27 September the equipment was covered with a tarpaulin. The ship left port in thick fog to elude British scouting units, and exercises were subsequently held in the Canaries/Azores area with the tanker *August Schultze*, the naval oiler *Samland* and *U 25*, *U 27* and *U 30*, but the German force was constantly shadowed by British warships, including the battlecruiser *Hood*. After the weather cleared, the ship exercised in the Bay of Cadiz with *U 27*, *U 30* and other units, also calling at Santa Cruz de la Palma (9 October), Cadiz (11th), Tangier (13th) and Gibraltar (15th) before returning to Germany on 20 October in company with *Admiral Graf Spee*. Between 7 and 12 November *Deutschland* took part in gunnery exer-

cises in the Baltic. In the period from May 1933 to the summer of 1938, the ship had cruised 130,000nm.

1939

Gunnery exercises were carried out between 6 and 26 February with visits to Tenerife, La Palma and El Ferrol. Hitler boarded at Swinemünde on 23 March for a voyage to Memel at the time of its restoration into the German Reich. *Deutschland* joined other fleet units at Wilhelmshaven on 1 April for the launch of the battleship *Tirpitz*. On 17 April she formed part of the first and only large-scale German foreign naval exercise when she accompanied the battlecruiser *Gneisenau*, flagship of Fleet C-in-C Admiral Carls, the 3rd Destroyer Division, the 6th and 7th U-boat Flotillas, the U-boat tender *Erwin Wassner* and the oiler *Samland*. During the manoeuvres a massed U-boat attack was demonstrated. Ports visited were Vigo and Malaga, with a crew excursion to Granada. *Deutschland* berthed at Wilhelmshaven on 16 May and participated in naval exercises in the Baltic between 12 and 16 June, including the usual flag-showing off seaside resorts, following which the ship docked at Wilhelmshaven for strengthening work to the foundations of Motor Rooms II and III.

On 21 August *Admiral Graf Spee* sailed from Wilhelmshaven, and at 0130 the next day the *Altmark* class naval oiler *Westerwald*, assigned to *Deutschland*, left for the Atlantic. *Deutschland* was still in the stationary trials anchorage near Gate 12 of the Navy Yard. That day four supplementary officers reported and an Ar 196 shipboard floatplane was delivered to replace the old He 60. On the 23rd five prize crew captains, wireless monitoring (B-Dienst) personnel, four radar petty officers and a meteorologist joined the ship's company, repair work was terminated and live ammunition was shipped. At 1430 on 24 August the engine room was given notice for 17.5kt, and *Deutschland* sailed for the appointed North Atlantic holding position off Cape Farewell an hour later. War watch conditions were introduced at 1900 when navigation lanterns were extinguished. Intensive battle training occupied the ship's company during the time spent off Greenland. On 30 August the Panzerschiff was provisioned and refuelled by *Westerwald*, after which the two ships practised various methods of bearing- and rangefinding. At 1800 on 31 August the following signal was received: '1. Commence hostilities against Poland in home waters 1.9.39 at 0445 hrs. 2. Attitude Western Powers unknown. 3. If Western Powers declare war own naval forces commence hostilities only in self-defence and if specifically ordered. 4. Panzerschiffe Atlantic, U-boats remain in waiting positions for the time being, even against Polish merchant traffic no hostile action at this time.' This signal was followed at 1745 on 1 September by: 'Britain and France have ordered general mobilisation. Further attitude still unclear. Italy will remain neutral in all cases.' War was declared on Germany by Britain, and later France, on 3 September. The ship's company was addressed by the commander during the evening and the situation was explained.

On the morning of the 5th the shipboard aircraft failed to return but was sighted and recovered by chance several hours later. A signal (FT 1621) at 1700 rom SKL stated: 'Restrained demeanour France and still hesitant war policy Britain make deployment Panzerschiffe presently inexpedient. 2. In view discernible cessation enemy merchant traffic and presumed planned search for Panzerschiffe, present deployment unfavourable and undesirable with regard to prospects for success. 3. Commerce warfare suspended, remain waiting positions remote from operational areas. Respects North Atlantic, South Atlantic, Indian Ocean. Radio silence!' *Deutschland* refuelled from *Westerwald* on the 11th and 17th of the month and shipped provisions on the 20th, the intervening period being used for battle training.

On 27 September *Deutschland* received the following orders:

1. Resume commerce warfare according operational orders by attacks in operational area. Previous special orders respecting France lifted. Proceed as against Britain.
2. SKL assumes *Deutschland* North Atlantic, *Admiral Graf Spee* South Atlantic. If correct do not signal but operate in intended operational area.
3. Report position and intentions on contact with enemy warships or if reported by merchant shipping.

Deutschland's anti-shipping sortie was not crowned with success. Two freighters were sunk – the British *Stonegate* east of Bermuda on 5 October and the Norwegian *Lorentz W. Hansen* east of Newfoundland on the 14th – while others were stopped, searched and allowed to proceed. An international incident developed following the seizure on 9 October of the US freighter *City of Flint* for alleged contraband. *Stonegate*'s crew were transferred aboard and an 18-strong prize party under Leutnant Pussbach took over control and set off for Germany. The *City of Flint* called in for fuel and water at Tromsø, where the Norwegian authorities released the *Stonegate* prisoners. As Pussbach had inadequate charts he went to

Murmansk, but he returned to Tromsø on 30 October to protests from the US Government. Pussbach was informed that he could pass through Norwegian waters but must not anchor. On 3 November he anchored at Haugesund on the orders of the German Vice-Consul and was promptly deprived of command, the prize crew being interned. The *City of Flint* was then restored to her original master by the Norwegian authorities.

The lack of sinkings by *Deutschland* was attributable to atrocious weather, the reintroduction of the convoy system by the British and the re-routing of traffic with effect from the outbreak of war. On the credit side, the mere presence of German raiders on the sea lanes caused the enemy to take extensive counter-measures: between 21 and 30 October, for example, on the Antilles–Channel route, the French Navy had deemed it necessary to employ the battleship *Dunkerque*, three light cruisers and eight destroyers on convoy escort duties combined with maintaining the search for the German heavy unit.

The next meeting with *Westerwald* for refuelling and re-provisioning lasted two days in a severe storm. *Deutschland* had sustained major damage: splits had appeared in the superstructure and Motor Rooms II, III and IV were repeatedly out of action as seas poured down the poorly positioned ventilation ports. The operation had to be abandoned and *Deutschland* headed for home. In the breakthrough she encountered a hurricane and rolled up to 30 degrees. The motor rooms were frequently unserviceable, although the engine-room personnel were able to cope with the problems.

On 14 November the ship was met by the destroyers *Friedrich Eckholdt*, *Friedrich Ihn*, *Bruno Heinemann* and *Erich Steinbrinck* and at 0600 the next morning the pilot vessel *Rugard* led the cruiser through the Great Belt. Off the lightship *Fehmarn Belt*, Admiral Carls, C-in-C Naval Group East, transferred aboard from the destroyer *Anton Schmitt* and on 16 November *Deutschland* dropped anchor at Gotenhafen.

In the former Polish port the commander was promoted to Konteradmiral and replaced by Kapitän zur See August Thiele. Throughout the German Navy for the duration of the war an issue of cap tallies bearing the word 'Kriegsmarine' was made. On 15 November the War Diary records the renaming of the ship *Lützow*, although the instruction had been noted in the signal log before *Deutschland* entered Norwegian waters. Acccording to legend, Hitler initiated the change of name to avoid the psychological and propaganda implications should a ship with the name '*Deutschland*' be sunk. However, the recommendation in fact originated with Grossadmiral Raeder. In a statement about the matter he said:

'The reasons which persuaded me to recommend to the Führer that the name "*Deutschland*" should be changed to "*Lützow*" are the following:

'1. The return of the Panzerschiff *Deutschland* to home waters and the evacuation of the North Atlantic area of operations by German surface units must be concealed from the enemy for as long as possible in order that enemy forces tied down there by her assumed presence should remain and so effectively free *Graf Spee* for her activities in the South Atlantic and Indian Oceans. The change of name is favoured in view of the secrecy of this purpose.

'2. It is intended to sell the heavy cruiser *Lützow* to the USSR. It is desirable that this fact is concealed for as long as possible. The change of name is helpful for camouflaging the purpose.

'3. The need continually to deploy the Panzerschiffe compels us to accept the possibility that eventually one of them may fall victim to a superior enemy force. On the one hand, it would be a highly undesirable psychological blow to the Kriegsmarine and the whole German people; and on the other hand it would be a welcome opportunity for the enemy to make political capital of the fact that an Panzerschiff with the name '*Deutschland*' had been sunk by them. It is proper to change the name and so avoid the general psychological effect that such a loss would entail.'

On 25 January 1940, in an announcement intended to 'disinform', the OKM reported: 'The Panzerschiff *Deutschland*, which has been engaged in commerce warfare in Atlantic waters since the outbreak of war, has recently returned to Germany. The Führer and Supreme Commander of the Wehrmacht has ordered the Panzerschiff *Deutschland* to be renamed "heavy cruiser *Lützow*", since the name "*Deutschland*" is to be reserved for a larger ship. The heavy cruiser originally launched with the name "*Lützow*" is also to be renamed.'*

At 1400 on 21 November *Lützow* sailed from Gotenhafen and anchored early next day in Wilhelmshaven roads, from where, at 1900 on the 24th, in company with the light cruisers *Leipzig* (flagship of Konteradmiral Lütjens) and *Köln*, the destroyers *Bernd von Arnim*, *Karl Galster*, *Friedrich Ihn* and *Bruno Heinemann* and torpedo-boats of the 6th Flotilla, she made a brief excursion to the Skagerrak on an anti-contraband patrol, returning to anchor at Wilhelms-

haven the next day. On the 26th *Lützow* entered the inner harbour and moored alongside quay A4 until the 28th, when she left for Gotenhafen via the Kiel Canal. The purpose of these movements was to conceal the sailing of the battlecruisers *Scharnhorst* and *Gneisenau*.

In December the ship entered the Danzig yard for a refit with a view to undertaking a second Atlantic mission scheduled for mid-February 1940. The crew were meanwhile quartered aboard the former luxury liner *Pretoria*.

1940

The ship's company reboarded on 21 January, and during the next week engine trials were run over the measured mile despite the hindrance of coastal ice. Live ammunition was shipped on 31 January and fitting-out was completed. On 15 February the OKW report of 25 January 1940 announcing the renaming of the ship and the reclassification of the two remaining units of the class as heavy cruisers was officially released.

Battle training took place off Gotenhafen from 16 to 27 February, and from the 28th a full programme, including torpedo, gunnery and searchlight practice, commenced, during the course of which the starboard propeller was damaged by ice, causing the remainder of the exercises to be run at 12kt.

Together with the light cruiser *Emden* and the oiler *Nordmark*, *Lützow* entered the frozen port of Swinemünde on 12 March and was soon ice-bound. On the 14th the ship was removed to floating dock B at Kiel, where the damaged propeller was replaced. The cruiser's anti-mine gear was tested on 25 and 26 March and gunnery exercises were resumed. Orders had been received on 6 February for a second Atlantic commerce-raiding operation, and for this purpose *Lützow* moved to anchorage A4 at Wilhelmshaven on 4 April. But other priorities now supervened.

[*Translator's note:* Germany depended on supplies of Scandinavian iron ore imported in her freighters loading at Narvik. It was the (legitimate) practice of these ships to make their way southwards through Norwegian coastal waters so as to afford themselves immunity from attack under international law. Following the earlier incidents involving the *City of Flint* and *Westerwald*, the storming of the *Altmark* at Jössingfjord on 16 February was the last

---

* By coincidence, *Deutschland*'s *Altmark* class naval oiler *Westerwald* was renamed *Nordmark* following a diplomatic incident with the Norwegian authorities during her passage home in late November.

straw. In the subsequent diplomatic exchanges, Norway had condemned the British action as illegal. However, as she had instructed her warships at the time to observe the incident and not interfere, Hitler deduced that Norway would not protect his iron-ore freighters when the first incidents occurred and so invasion was essential.]

Lützow was urgently needed in support of Operation 'Weserübung', the occupation of Denmark and Norway, and was allocated to Group 2 to seize Trondheim. At the last moment auxiliary motor 1 broke down and the ship had to be reallocated to Group 5 for Oslo. Once her 450-strong contingent of Army occupation troops had embarked, the ship made for Kiel on 7 April and anchored in the Förde overnight before setting off in convoy for Norway on the 8th. Group 5 was under the command of Vizeadmiral Kummetz aboard his flagship, the new and not fully worked up *Blücher*, the other units being *Lützow*, the light cruiser *Emden*, the torpedo-boats *Möwe*, *Kondor* and *Albatros*, eight R-boats and two converted whale-catchers. The British C-in-C, Vice-Admiral Horton, had ordered all available submarines of the 2nd, 3rd and 6th British and 10th French Flotillas to take up positions in the Kattegat and Skagerrak and along the south-west coast of Norway to protect the impending British landings in Norway, the British being unaware at that point of the German invasion. For the German units there were numerous false alarms on the way, although at 1906, off Skagen, HM Submarine *Trident* managed to get within range but failed to hit *Lützow* with any of her complement of ten torpedoes.

When wireless monitors aboard *Lützow* took down a Norwegian radio announcement at 2325 that all coastal lights were to be doused, the cruiser signalled this information to Konteradmiral Kummetz together with the commander's proposal that *Lützow* should go on ahead to penetrate the dangerous Dröbak Narrows at high speed before the black-out came into effect, but the suggestion was disregarded.

In Oslofjord at 7kt on account of the darkness, *Lützow* was in line astern of *Blücher* and at battle stations. Approaching Dröbak Narrows at dawn in drifting mist, speed was increased to 12kt, but *Blücher*, illuminated from both banks of the fjord by heavy searchlight batteries, was soon being pounded by 28cm shells (and, later, torpedoes) at a range of about 500m. On seeing this, Kapitän zur See Thiele had given the order to reply, the port side medium battery under the command of No 2 Gunnery Officer opening fire at a range of 1.8km. Shortly before 'A' turret could engage, *Lützow* sustained three 15cm hits.

The first shell struck the upper side of 'A' turret's centre barrel near the crenel shutter. The pressure wave lifted the turret roof by a few millimetres, allowing splinters to penetrate the interior. The cradle for the right barrel collapsed. Cabling and other instruments were shredded, and the barrel resetting apparatus, the hydraulic installation and the main turning motor were put out of action. Four turret crewmen were slightly wounded. The second shell struck near Frame 135, Compartment XIII. The shell had a flat trajectory and entered the 'tween deck through a porthole. It exploded on passing through the ship's side, gouging a tear 1m in length. A traverse frame was damaged and the hospital isolation room and upper deck pierced, the latter in three places. Fifteen holes were counted in the bulkhead dividing Compartments XII and XIII. The hospital operating theatre and WC block were damaged. Fires were extinguished in the ship's hospital and upper deck Compartment XIII. Two Army personnel were killed and six badly wounded. One doctor and one crewman were seriously wounded. The third shell struck the port crane, splinters spraying 26m in all directions as far as the funnel platform. The ship's reserve aircraft was damaged, searchlight cables were ripped and a fire started among the AA ready ammunition. Three men died in Port III 15cm gunhouse and two were wounded; the battery officer, one petty officer and five ratings were wounded in Port IV 15cm gunhouse; and one man died and one was slightly wounded at the port AA battery. In addition, two magazine ratings and one searchlight rating were wounded.

Lützow had also been raked by cannon and machine-gun fire. Seeing the hopeless plight of the flagship, Thiele ordered Lützow full astern out of the danger area while smoke from the fire below decks continued to envelop the ship. The damage control party succeeded in extinguishing the fire in Compartment XIII 'tween deck and hospital at 0459. The sealing of splinter and bullet holes took twenty minutes. It was found that a splinter from a near-miss had slashed open trim tank XII 4.4 20cm below the waterline.

'A' turret's right barrel was restored after five minutes; the left barrel was working again after 30 minutes by the use of electrical and later hydraulic leverage gear. The centre barrel remained unserviceable. The shipboard AA fired at various targets until 0543, when the ship was sufficiently clear of the danger area to turn in mid-stream and head down-fjord.

The experience served to confirm the virtual impossibility for even large warships to cope with well-sited and concealed shore gun and torpedo emplacements. *Blücher* had lost the use of her foretop in the first few moments of the action and controlled fire was subsequently only possible from the shipboard AA. She capsized and sank with the loss of about 300 lives at 0732 that morning, 9 April 1940. Kapitän zur See Thiele, aboard *Lützow*, assumed command of Group 5 following the loss of the flagship and disembarked troops down-fjord at Sonsbukten for a land assault on the Dröbak defences and Oslo. Coastal emplacements were bombarded before the Group withdrew to the naval base at Horten. Dröbak was secured by German troops that evening, the garrison not being required to lower the Norwegian flag out of respect for their military achievement. At 0845 on 10 April *Lützow*, *Emden*, *Möwe* and the minor vessels passed through Dröbak and, under pilotage, made fast at Vippetange Quay, Oslo, at 1145.

At 1540 the same afternoon *Lützow* sailed for Kiel for repairs and to fit out for the still-scheduled Atlantic commerce-raiding operation. Along the fjord she made stops to pick up and set down various passengers before releasing her two escorts, *Möwe* and *Kondor*, to assist their sister vessel *Albatros*, aground and sinking near Söstrene, at 2200.

On entering the Skagerrak, the cruiser found a northeast wind Force 4, Sea State 3, on a clear starry night with exceptional visibility. *Lützow* was soon steering 117° at 24kt, Thiele remarking in the War Diary that, as British submarines were known to be stationed along the Swedish coast, he proposed to give them ample sea room by 'standing off a little to the west at high speed'. At 0020 on 11 April the heavy cruiser passed the Skagen–Paternoster line on course 138°, from which point the War Diary recounts the sorry story:

0120: Radar reports object astern at 6°, 1.5km.
0126: Turned to port at 1.15km. Nothing seen, no further radar contacts, starboard rudder to original bearing to get us through Skagen Narrows as soon as possible.
0129: Ship still turning. Enormous shock astern. Torpedo track reported acute angle port side. Assume submarine attack.
0130: Ship still turning, rudder jammed starboard 20°. Compartment II does not answer or obey engine telegraph. Reported to bridge, 'Manual rudder room cannot be manned. Stern flooding, ship listing to port and gradually settling.' I intend to steer by propellers, port astern, starboard forward, at 18kt.

HM Submarine *Spearfish* had fired a fan of her last four torpedoes at *Lützow* and obtained a single hit astern, knocking off both screws and the rudder and breaking the stern.

0220: Signal to Group East: 'My position is 233°, 10 nautical miles off Skagen. Am unmanoeuvrable, flooding held, both screws lost. *Lützow* situation: ship drifting broadside to sea at 2kt SW towards Skagen. I hope to find a lee and calm waters in Aalbäck Bay. As the ship is visible from afar, further submarine attacks are to be expected. Boats made ready for lowering, all crew members wearing lifejackets, all lower decks evacuated with exception of damage control personnel. 'B' turret has jettisoned all ammunition to help lighten the stern. All Flak guns closed up, sharp anti-submarine watch set.
0318: Sent off ObltzS V. in the motor cutter to Skagen to request tugs and escort vessels.
0305 to 0337: Signals from Group East, 'Torpedo-boats *Luchs*, *Seeadler*, *Jaguar*, *Falke*, *Möwe* [and] *Kondor*, 17th UJ Flotilla, 2nd E-boat Flotilla and *UJ 172* on way to assist.

At 0340 the ship's launch was set down to circle the stricken cruiser 'as anti-submarine protection' and at 0433 the first vessels of 17th UJ Flotilla hove into sight, to be joined at 0500 by the 19th Minesweeping Flotilla. Some of the ship's company was then transferred off and *Lützow* was taken in tow. A few minutes later 'ObltzS V.' returned from shore in company with numerous fishing vessels and the Skagen lifeboat.

The cruiser had 1,300 tonnes of seawater below decks and a 12m draught astern, which led to a number of groundings. As the wind and sea began to rise, it was feared that the stern section, attached to the rest of the ship by the two screw-less drive shafts, would drop off at the Compartment III/IV bulkhead. The Danish tug *Garm* took the towing hawser and at 1420 the tugs *Wotan* and *Seeteufel* joined the group, *Norder* and *Thor* promising to arrive by the morning of the 12th.

The salvage team and *Lützow* eventually made the Deutsche Werke yard at Kiel at 2022 on 14 April. The repairs would last well into 1941. The Norwegian operation cost the cruiser 19 dead – four at Dröbak, buried in Oslo, and 15 when the torpedo struck, also interred with full military honours, at Kiel.

When surveyed in drydock, the extent of the damage surpassed the worst fears. The gash between the aftership and the remainder of the hull was extremely large and on the starboard side the armoured deck above the armour belt was ripped. The affected area below the waterline was just mangled steel. A long lay-up under repair was indicated and the ship was accordingly decommissioned on 8 August, only a small detail plus the Flak personnel remaining aboard. Fregattenkapitän Fritz Krauss acted as caretaker-commander from April to June and the position was vacant from June to August, when Kapitänleutnant Heller took control of the ship's business until March 1941.

During this repair in drydock *Lützow* received a new stern, propellers, shafts and rudder, and other modifications included a platform on the battle-mast for radar equipment and an additional observation post at the foretop.

On three nights in early July Kiel was the target for RAF raids, and on the 9th *Lützow* was hit on the starboard side near 'A' turret, Frame 142/143, by a large bomb which penetrated to the 'tween deck, where it failed to explode.

On 18 November an S-Anlage (an AEG remote-controlled active hydrophone installation, developed in 1940) was fitted. On 5 December the cruiser moved to an anchorage and on the 16th of the month the accommodation decks were declared ready for occupation.

1941

'A' turret received a new gun cradle and centre barrel during the period 1–20 January, and on the 21st trials were run with the port engine. By 1 February all crew rooms were ready for habitation, and gunnery co-ordination work commenced from 21 March. A trial run was made on the 28th and the radio equipment was charged up the following day.

Lützow was recommissioned by Kapitän zur See Leo Kreisch on 31 March without undue fuss and the cruiser was at sea the same day for signals trials before embarking on weeks of working up for the Atlantic commerce-raiding cruise postponed from April 1940 and which was now scheduled to proceed in June with Trondheim as the jumping-off point. The naval oiler *Uckermark* (ex *Altmark*) and the supply ship *Egerland* had been earmarked for replenishment duties. Sister-ship *Admiral Scheer* and her oiler *Nordmark*, recently returned from a long and successful operation in the South Atlantic and Indian Oceans, had also been given notice for a repeat operation to commence one month after the *Lützow*'s departure.

For the SKL to persist with such bold ideas after the loss of *Bismarck* in the North Atlantic on 27 May was highly questionable. Following their successful Atlantic operation in February and March, the battlecruisers

Scharnhorst and *Gneisenau* were bottled up in Brest, where they were joined on 1 June by the heavy cruiser *Prinz Eugen*, whose commander had been adroit enough to elude the large naval force rounding up the chain of German tankers and supply ships in the wake of the *Bismarck* disaster. These three heavy units had no chance of engaging in further Atlantic activities because of growing Allied air supremacy over the seas.

By mid-1941 it was already clear that everything now depended on the U-boat Arm. A few raiders in the guise of merchant ships were experiencing continued success, but their days were numbered. Thus the wisdom of sending forth the two surviving former Panzerschiffe, whose only advantage was their enormous range, must be seriously called into question.

Operation 'Sommerreise' (Summer Cruise) began on 12 June when *Lützow* left Kiel for Norway with the destroyers *Z 23*, *Z 24*, *Hans Lody*, *Friedrich Eckholdt* and *Karl Galster* as escorts. *U 79* and *U 559* scouted ahead for the group. Before the voyage began the B-Dienst had reported intense activity by the RAF on 10 and 11 June, indicating that the intended sailing was known to the enemy. The German convoy remained undetected in the Kattegat and Skagerrak, but shortly after midnight on the 13th the B-Dienst alerted the commander to enemy shadowers.

The group was under the protection of a Luftwaffe umbrella, but the usual communication difficulties existed between ships and aircraft. An RAF Beaufort torpedo-bomber, a type similar to the German Bf 110, had established the German recognition signal and been accepted into the Luftwaffe escort. Off Egersund the British aircraft swooped down to within 600m of *Lützow*, released its torpedo and escaped.

The torpedo hit the cruiser, travelling at 21kt, on the port side of Frame 82 in the torpedo bulkhead above the stabiliser keel. On the other side of the bulkhead was Motor Room (port) II. A violent shock was felt throughout the ship, which took on an immediate list. The drive room was severely damaged and both diesels were dislodged. All motors stopped and all electrical plant failed. The ship drifted out of control, black smoke billowing through all rooms from the damaged smoke-making apparatus in the stern. Fortunately for *Lützow*, the smoke swiftly enveloped the ship and the second British aircraft arriving to deliver the coup de grâce was unable to see the target and the torpedo ran wide. Without electrical power it was impossible to adjust the trim or institute compensatory flooding until power was restored in one electrical plant, and the cruiser remained with a 21-degree list until the following morning. Magazine VII 7.1 was flooded when threatened by the fire in Drive Room I.

The initial damage reports confirmed that the generators in electrical plants 2 and 3 were flooded and all others threatened and that cables in Drive Room I and Motor Room II were torn out of the torpedo bulkhead and short-circuiting. After provisional repairs, the cruiser headed for Kiel on one shaft at 16kt with all watertight doors and hatches shut. By 1100 she had a second electrical plant functioning.

At Kiel, *Lützow* entered Deutsche Werke Drydock VI for repairs that would last over six months. A survey of the damage at the shipyard revealed that the stabiliser keel, hull wall, inner and outer wall passage bulkheads and transverse bulkhead 83 were seriously holed and split; in the armoured deck, frames in the vicinity of the hit, ground vent VII 4.2. and a hydrant pipe in Compartment VIII had been destroyed; the 'tween deck had been distorted upwards and the torpedo bulkhead severely dented; and the wall passages between Frames 62 and 94, the double bottom between Frames 72 and 94 and the 'tween deck from Frames 55 to 105 had been flooded. Elsewhere, the AA direction centre and command relay installation had been knocked out by the shock of the detonation, with instruments unserviceable; the rotator motors for searchlights II, III and IV were out of action and in any case no searchlight had electrical power; the surface gunnery command relay system was partially out of commission; two electrical plants were completely unserviceable and the two main turrets had intermittent supplies of current only; and the ammunition hoists for 15cm guns I and VII were flooded.

In July Kapitän zur See Rudolf Stange was appointed the cruiser's seventh commander.

During the night of 7 September Wohnboot III, which housed the cruiser's secretarial offices with all secret files and other documents dating from 1 January 1939 was completely destroyed during an RAF air raid on Kiel. On 22 September 'Training Company *Lützow*' was set up ashore under Kapitänleutnant Köhler; it consisted of five officers, eleven warrant officers, 41 NCOs and 389 lower rates. During the absence of Kapitän zur See Stange, Kapitän zur See Leo Kreisch was acting commander from September 1941 to January 1942. Flak, damage control and some engine room personnel remained aboard the ship while she was undergoing repairs. *Lützow* survived unscathed a number of heavy air attacks on Kiel and its naval dockyard, the worst of which occurred on 30 September and during the nights of 23 and 24 October.

1942

At the beginning of January the repairs were nearing completion, despite increasing enemy air supremacy, and *Lützow* loaded ammunition, carried out inclination tests, tested her anti-mine gear, charged up the radio installations and so forth, and on 17 January she emerged from the shipyard, sailing the next day for Gotenhafen for working up. Heavy icing in the Baltic interfered with these plans, and after sustaining propeller damage in an ice-field *Lützow* laid up at Swinemünde. By April the situation had not eased appreciably, and even an appointment to have a new radar unit installed at Danzig on the 2nd had to be postponed until the 10th because of the weather. On 21 April Grossadmiral Raeder inspected ship and crew prior to a programme of radar, mine clearance and gunnery exercises in combination with destroyers, U-boats and aircraft. On 10 May the cruiser reported herself battle-ready, and on the 12th she left Swinemünde for the Baltic island of Bornholm as a staging post for the run to Norway. On 15 May she fell in behind the mine destructor ship *Sperrbrecher 13* and, escorted by the destroyers *Z 29* and *Richard Beitzen* (and later *Z 27* and *Hans Lody*) and the fleet escort ship *F 1*, set out northwards. The group was shadowed by British radar all the way, but despite frequent air and submarine alarms no attack materialised.

At 0520 on 17 May the convoy anchored in daylight at Kravenesfjord near Kristiansand. The cruiser sailed at nightfall, escorted by *Z 27*, *Z 29* and *Richard Beitzen*. The submarine danger off the western Norwegian coast was particularly acute, and enemy reconnaissance flights were almost continuous. When spotted off Bergen, the group sheltered at an anchorage in Grimstadfjord and continued at nightfall, the escort strengthened by the torpedo-boat *T 15*.

At 0615 on 19 May *Lützow* moored inside a box of anti-torpedo nets at Lofjord near Trondheim. On the 24th of the month she resumed course for Narvik with *Z 27*, *Z 29*, *Richard Beitzen*, *T 7*, five E-boats and the naval oiler *Nordmark* in attendance and at 2345 that night anchored in Bogen Bay, where she found an assembly comprising her sister-ship *Admiral Scheer*, the floating Flak battery *Nymphe*, *Z 24*, *Z 28*, *Z 30*, *T 5*, *T 7*, the naval oiler *Dithmarschen*, the supply ship *Pelagos* and the E-boat depot ship *Tanga*.

On 4 June these ships were designated No 2 Battle Group with *Lützow* as the flagship of Vizeadmiral Kummetz, BdK (C-in-C Cruisers). Exercises were held with *Admiral Scheer* from 8 to 10 June inclusive, but on the 11th *Lützow* was back in her nets. The chronic fuel shortage required strict economies, and only sporadic exercises were possible. This led to a request to Admiral Northern Waters by Kapitän zur See Stange for a weekly 'exercise' fuel supplement of 100 cubic metres! This sly dig was symptomatic of serious differences of opinion between the ships' commanders and the BdK, who had not endeared himself to the former from the outset by putting ashore several veteran and valued officers to make space for a single Admiral Staff officer. This type of conduct – together with the endless idling within the torpedo nets – had a detrimental effect on the general shipboard climate and morale.

At the beginning of July an operation was announced to destroy Allied convoy PQ.17. Late on the 2nd of the month *Lützow*, *Admiral Scheer*, the destroyers *Z 24*, *Z 27*, *Z 28*, *Z 29*, *Z 30* and the naval oiler *Dithmarschen* raised anchor in Bogen Bay to make for a rendezvous with the battleship *Tirpitz* and other units. At 0242 on the 3rd *Lützow* grounded in Tjeldsund and assumed a list of 2–3 degrees. Trim tanks in Compartments XIII and VIII and fuel bunkers in the double bottom of Compartments IX and X had sprung leaks. After Kummetz had transferred his flag to *Admiral Scheer*, *Lützow* returned to Bogen Bay and at 0904 dropped anchor inside her nets, where divers found a 30cm dent in Compartments X and XI with rips and a number of popped rivets. Smaller holes about a metre above the keel were discovered (Compartments XIII–XII). Seven trim tanks in the outer wall passage, six bunkers and one waste oil tank in the double bottom had flooded, and about 290 cubic metres of seawater stood beneath three diesel motors and two drive rooms. The outer shell plating had damage over a length of about 70–80m. *Lützow* returned to the routine of air alarms, battle training at anchor and idling while awaiting the return of the battle group, but the participation of the regular warships had been cancelled and the convoy was left to aircraft and the U-boats.

After refuelling from *Dithmarschen* on 9 July, the cruiser set off for the first stage of the return home with *Z 24*, *Friedrich Ihn*, *T 7* and *T 15* as escorts, and entered Trondheim the next day on the port engine, the starboard engine having been shut down following pollution of the diesel fuel with lubricating oil through a leaking tank.

A month passed before *Lützow* left Lofjord on 9 August and, undetected despite numerous aircraft alarms, made fast at Swinemünde on the 12th. The cruiser unloaded her ammunition and fuel at Kiel shipyard the next day and was in Drydock VI on 31 August for repair. During the course of the work about 250 square metres of outer plating, including framing, was renewed between longitudinal Frames III and IV. The period was marked by a number of minor incidents: on 23 September there was a dockyard blaze; on the 27th there was a fire in magazine VII 8.1; the next day a fire occurred in a basket of papers; and on 3 November, after the ship had left dock, 'B' turret struck a floating crane while traversing, the left barrel being knocked 7mm out of true. Thirty-three per cent of the officers, 16 per cent of the NCOs and 18 per cent of the other rates had been replaced meanwhile. Half of the watchkeeping officers were new to the ship, as were 67 per cent of the watch engineers.

On 30 October the shipyard repairs were finally completed and, in company with the destroyers *ZH 1* and *Karl Galster*, *Lützow* left Kiel on 9 November for the eastern Baltic to begin trials and battle training off Cape Arkona. Gunnery practice followed a run over the measured mile on 4 November, and on the 8th the cruiser left Gotenhafen for Norway with the destroyers *Karl Galster*, *Theodor Riedel* and *Z 31* escorting. The group was shadowed and subjected to repeated attacks by aircraft. Having passed Egersund on the 10th, cruiser and destroyers arrived undamaged at Bogen Bay, Narvik, on the 12th, the single day's run to Altafjord being accomplished with *Z 31* and *Theodor Riedel* on the night of the 16th. Altafjord was the hide-out of the Group flagship, the heavy cruiser *Admiral Hipper*, the light cruisers *Nürnberg* and *Köln* and various smaller units. *Admiral Scheer* was released on *Lützow*'s arrival.

On Christmas Eve notice was given of impending Operation 'Regenbogen' (Rainbow) against Allied convoy JW.51B, which had been identified by air reconnaissance and the B-Dienst. On 30 December *Admiral Hipper*, *Lützow* and the destroyers *Richard Beitzen*, *Friedrich Eckholdt*, *Z 24*, *Z 30*, *Z 31* and *Theodor Riedel* sailed along the Norwegian coast before heading out to sea. The objective, the fourteen-ship Allied convoy, had sailed from Loch Ewe on 22 December, but the German admiral was unaware of the strength of its escort. Close in were the British destroyers *Onslow*, *Oribi*, *Obedient*, *Obdurate*, *Orwell* and *Achates*, the radar-equipped minesweeper *Bramble*, the corvettes *Rhododendron* and *Hyderabad* and two trawlers; as loose escort were the cruisers *Sheffield* and *Jamaica* and the destroyer *Opportune* plus, later, *Matchless*; and as distant escort were the battleship *Anson*, the heavy cruiser *Cumberland* and the destroyers *Forester*, *Impulsive* and *Icarus*. Lining the route out from Altafjord were the submarines *Trespasser*, *Seadog*, *Unruly* and *Graph*.

The general weather situation was extremely adverse. The whole operation was a disaster, and it was surely a tactical error to have spread the German force, which was apparently done in order to locate the convoy by means of a broad line of search (the line was 85nm long with *Admiral Hipper* at its northern end, *Lützow* at the southern end and the six destroyers in between). This put the German battle group in a weak position upon encountering the enemy escorts, which might have been expected but nevertheless came as a complete surprise. *Admiral Hipper* bore the brunt of the skirmish and received three hits, one of which did great damage in her boiler room.

The decisive factor in the fiasco was the vague and woolly wording of the operational orders issued by the shore command centres. The instructions were 'open on all sides' and ordered commanders to 'exercise restraint in the face of an equal enemy force, as acceptance of a greater risk is undesirable for the cruisers'. 'Greater risk' was qualified and explained as 'unnecessary risk': where the enemy force was stronger, commanders had to refuse battle. When *Lützow* eventually penetrated to within shooting distance of the merchant vessels of the convoy, the BdK signalled 'Break off action forthwith and retire to the west!'

The destroyer *Friedrich Eckholdt* was lost with all hands and *Admiral Hipper* was reduced to 15kt, while *Lützow* and the five surviving destroyers returned home undamaged. The British lost the destroyer *Achates* and the minesweeper *Bramble* and had three 'O' class destroyers damaged, all at the hands of *Admiral Hipper*. However, the operation was an utter failure since no merchant ship of the convoy was lost.

1943

On 1 January the units returning from the so-called Battle of the Barents Sea were at anchor in the Norwegian fjords. *Lützow* remained in northern Norway and alternated irregularly between Bogen Bay and Altafjord to confuse Allied air reconnaissance. The failure of Operation 'Regenbogen' had had its consequences. In a lecture delivered on 6 January at Führer HQ justifying his action, Hitler ordered the decommissioning of all heavy units, which he deprecated as 'worthless and useless'. This 'irreversible' order resulted in the resignation of Grossadmiral Raeder. He was replaced by Admiral Dönitz, who was promoted to Grossadmiral on appointment and who later managed to have the decommissioning order partially rescinded.

In March, on the arrival of *Tirpitz* and *Scharnhorst* at Bogen Bay, *Lützow* shifted to Altafjord. She was experiencing problems with her diesels, and on 20 July this led to the cancellation of Operation 'Husar' in the Kara Sea, which had been intended to emulate Operation 'Wunderland' carried out the previous year by *Admiral Scheer*. On 23 June the Fleet C-in-C and C-in-C Naval Group North, Generaladmiral Schniewind, visited the ship in company with the BdK, Admiral Kummetz. Later the cruiser exercised with *Tirpitz*, and on 5 July a general exercise was held involving all units of the group. *Lützow* was at full readiness on 9 July, and on the 13th and 14th of the month she exercised in company with the naval oiler *Nordmark*. On the 14th she also received notice of her impending return to Germany. The ship was required to be battleworthy at all times, and this could not be guaranteed because of the continuing engine problems. On occasion she was reduced to importuning an emergency power supply from the oiler *Dithmarschen* and the floating U-boat power stations *Watt*, *Wilhelm Brenner* and *Karl Junge*.

Once the diesels were serviceable again, *Lützow* resumed her part in Group exercises. There was no prospect of further anti-convoy operations as the Allies had suspended their USSR sailings because of the heavy German warship and U-boat presence in northern Norway, but at least this confirmed the validity of the 'fleet in being' strategy, for the threat posed had also compelled the Allies to keep their own substantial presence in the area.

On 6 September, when *Tirpitz* and *Scharnhorst* sortied to Spitzbergen for Operation 'Wunderland II', *Lützow* occupied the net defences vacated by *Tirpitz* in order to confuse Allied air reconnaissance. After the original stations were occupied on their return, *Tirpitz* was seriously damaged at Kaafjord in the attack by British X-craft on the 23rd, but *Lützow* was in a remote inlet and escaped attention. This was also the last day of her Norwegian sojourn as the decision had already been taken to return her to home waters. That night, in company with the destroyers *Erich Steinbrinck*, *Friedrich Ihn*, *Paul Jacobi* and *Z 27*, she began her voyage south in stages, on the 24th anchoring at Skömenfjord, on the 26th passing through the Arctic Circle and on the 28th arriving off Kristiansand, where *Z 27* and *Friedrich Ihn* were released and replaced by *Z 38*. German ships in the Skagerrak and Kattegat were now menaced by a combination of bombers, submarines and MTBs, but *Lützow* sailed through unmolested, and after releasing *Z 38* on the 29th ran into Kiel with *Paul Jacobi* and *Erich Steinbrinck* only.

On 1 October the cruiser called at Gotenhafen and then entered the shipyard at Libau, Gotenhafen no longer being secure against air attack since the introduction by the

Allies of long-range bombers whose radius of action allowed them to strike at almost any place in the Reich. On 9 October the USAAF attacked Gotenhafen and sank the hospital ship *Stuttgart*. Kapitän zur See Stange stepped down as commander in November 1943 and Fregattenkapitän Biesterfeld took over as acting commander.

1944

Kapitän zur See Knoke was appointed commander of *Lützow* in January. The overhaul lasted into February; standing trials were conducted on the 27th, and on 5 March the cruiser moved to an outer anchorage at Libau from where she ran sea trials. By the 11th the full war complement of 1,156 officers and men was aboard, and four days later the ship began working up – important since in February the ship had been designated part of the newly formed Fleet Training Group. The following weeks saw intensive training, the ship exercising both alone and in company with *Prinz Eugen*, *Admiral Scheer*, *Nürnberg*, *Emden*, torpedo-boats, E-boats, U-boats and the gunnery target ship *Hessen*.

In June the cruiser was at Gotenhafen, where shore bombardment was practised on the 16th. On the 24th, in company with *Prinz Eugen*, *T 3*, *T 4* and *T 12*, *Lützow* sailed to the rocky coast of south-west Finland for battle training and inspection, and on the 27th exercises were held in the Gulf of Finland. The reason for the visit to these waters was the feared withdrawal of Finland from the Axis alliance (as, in fact, soon occurred).

On 8 July *Lützow* was again at Gotenhafen, from where she made various Baltic excursions. On the occasion of the Fleet C-in-C Generaladmiral Schniewind relinquishing his post to Admiral Meendsen-Bohlken, *Lützow* took part in the last Naval Review of German warships. Both admirals were aboard the light cruiser *Nürnberg* to review the sail-past of most major units of the German Fleet – the heavy cruisers *Prinz Eugen*, *Admiral Hipper*, *Lützow* and *Admiral Scheer* and the light cruisers *Köln*, *Leipzig* and *Emden* (*Tirpitz* was by this time crippled in a Norwegian fjord).

In the following weeks *Lützow* alternated her moorings among the various Baltic ports as far as the Gulf of Riga, although the whole area was insecure, particularly with regard to aircraft. The aerial threat grew steadily: enemy dive-bombers were now fitted with armour, making them much less vulnerable to the German 2cm Flak. For this reason *Lützow* exchanged two 3.7cm twin- and six 2cm single-mounted Flak for eight (later reduced to six, two

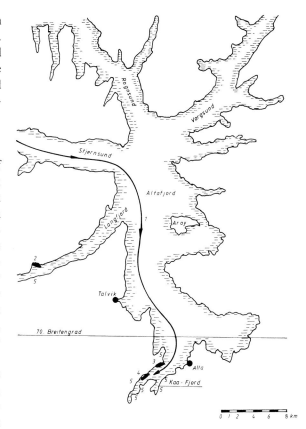

Above: The hide-out of the German heavy units in Norway at the time of the X-craft attack in 1943.
Key: (1) Course of British X-craft (only the attack on *Tirpitz* succeeded). (2) Anchorage of *Lützow* inside net defences. (3) Anchorage of *Scharnhorst* in net defences. (4) Anchorage of *Tirpitz* in net defences. (5) Flak installations.

having apparently been sabotaged) 4cm single and six 2cm twin mountings at Gotenhafen shipyard on 9 August.

Since 28 July, together with units of the Training Group (including *Prinz Eugen*), *Lützow* had been part of No 2 Battle Group under Konteradmiral Thiele. Between 22 and 25 September she and other units were in Finnish waters to protect German land units falling back following the departure of Finland from the Axis alliance. On the 27th, at Gotenhafen, the cruiser received two more 4cm AA guns, and she was in action again in October, bombarding Soviet land forces at Memel and near the Sworbe peninsula. In one day she fired 304 rounds of 28cm, 292 rounds of 15cm, 282 rounds of 10.5cm, 121 rounds of 4cm, 56 rounds of 3.7cm and 1,501 rounds of 2cm. Shooting was sporadic and largely directed by the Army ashore. The various

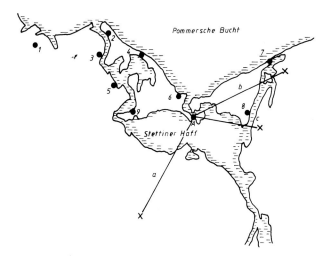

Above: Shore bombardment by *Lützow*'s main armament from the ship's last anchorage.
Key: A = Ship abandoned and scuttled. (1) Greifswald. (2) Peenemünde. (3) Wolgast. (4) Koserow. (5) Lassan. (6) Swinemünde. (7) Dievenow. (8) Wollin. (9) Usedam. X = targets during shore bombardment of Soviet bridgeheads, armour and troop assembly areas: Pasewalk (a), Cammin (b) and Pribbenow (c).

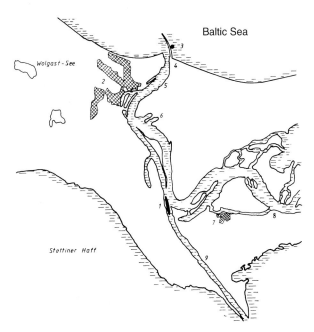

Above: The final anchorage, Kaiser Canal, Swinemünde.
Key. (1) *Lützow* abandoned and scuttled. (2) Town of Swine. (3) Lighthouse at harbour approach. (4) Eastern emergency harbour. (5) Ostswine. (6) Harbour basin. (7) Kaseburg. (8) Alte Swine. (9) Kaiser Canal.

naval units involved in this operation worked in shifts, the relieved ships returning to Gotenhafen to re-arm. Sworbe had already fallen when *Lützow* arrived to relieve *Admiral Scheer* on 23 November. Kapitän zur See Böhmig had temporary command of the ship during November. Eight hundred and twenty-four tonnes of explosive rained down on Gotenhafen on 18 December, but *Lützow* escaped damage and moved to Pillau towards the end of the month.

1945

From February, *Lützow*, *Admiral Scheer* and *Prinz Eugen* worked a rota for the shore bombardment of Soviet forces in East Prussia. On 13 January the expected but – at the highest level – underestimated major Russian offensive encountered weak German defences, which nevertheless fought on desperately, hindered by endless streams of refugees heading westwards towards the apparent salvation of the coast. On 8 February *Lützow*, escorted by *T 8*, *T 28* and *T 33*, bombarded Soviet advance columns off Frauenburg-Elbing and re-armed at Swinemünde on the 6th and 7th before returning to East Prussian waters. On 23 March the cruiser took part in the defence of Gotenhafen, Oxhöfter Kämpe and Hela and on 8 April put into Swinemünde to re-arm. The ship survived an air raid unscathed on the 13th, but a five-ton bomb dropped by a British Lancaster which achieved a near-miss on the 16th opened up 30m of the ship's side and she assumed a 56-degree list. Two 1,000lb bombs which hit the forward and aft 28cm magazines failed to explode.

With the help of salvage vessels the ship was restored to an even keel before electrical plant 4, the starboard 15cm gunhouses and 'A' turret were pumped dry. The guns were tested on 28 April, after which 'A' turret resumed the bombardment of Soviet land forces. The last commander of *Lützow*, Fregattenkapitän Ernst Lange, was appointed this month: by this time only gunnery personnel remained aboard the cruiser, the remainder having been landed on 17 April and formed into infantry 'emergency' units. Once all ammunition had been expended and it was clear that the situation could not improve, the order was given to scuttle the ship. Charges were set on 3/4 May but were detonated prematurely by a shipboard fire.

The eventual fate of the wreck is not known. She was said to have been seen in 1948–49 at Kronstadt (which is doubtful: confusion with the *Admiral Hipper* class heavy cruiser *Lützow*, sold to the USSR in 1940, is likely). Other sources report that she capsized and sank off Kolberg while under tow.

Above: The former armoured frigate/central-battery ironclad *Deutschland* – seen here as a 7,645-ton large cruiser after major rebuilding – makes a transit of the Kiel Canal some time between 1897 and 1904. Launched at the Samuda Brothers' Yard, London, in 1874, she remained in service until 1906 and was the first warship to bear the name.

Below: The 13,200-ton pre-dreadnought *Deutschland*, the second warship so named, was the Fleet flagship from September 1906. Launched at Kiel in November 1904, she carried four 28cm guns as her main armament and was capable of 18kt. Although the class was obsolete on entering service, her two sister-ships, *Schlesien* and *Schleswig-Holstein*, remained in commission until 1945. *Deutschland* was at Jutland but was afterwards relegated to coast defence duties and scrapped in 1922. This prewar photograph was taken during Navy manouevres. The ship flies the Kaiser's standard, indicating his presence aboard.

Panzerkreuzer Deutschland
(in Erwartung
des Stapellaufs!)

Above: A bow view of Panzerschiff 'A' as numerous spectators arrive for the launching ceremony.
Left: The hull on the slipway seen from astern.

Right: *Deutschland* was launched on 19 May 1931 at the Deutsche Werke yard, Kiel. Here the guests of honour are seen arriving: from the left, Reich President Paul von Hindenburg, wearing the Imperial uniform of a General Field Marshal; the Commanding Officer of the Baltic Naval Station, Vizeadmiral Hansen; Reich Chancellor Dr Brüning; and the Chief of the Naval Staff, Admiral Raeder.

Below: To the strains of *Deutschland über Alles* and cheered by an assembled multitude estimated at 60,000, *Deutschland* takes the water a little earlier than planned: the hull rumbled off as Hindenburg was preparing to deliver his christening speech, tearing away the cable network to the microphones.

Left, upper: *Deutschland*'s hull, festooned with garlands and dressed overall, is launched into its element.

Left, lower: Having brought the hull to a standstill, tugs begin the tow to the quayside of the fitting-out basin.

Right, top: *Deutschland* fitting out. This view of 'A' turret forward of amidships shows a crane lowering one of the 28cm barrels into its cradle.

Right, centre: All three barrels of 'A' turret are now in place and an armoured plate for the turret roof is being lowered into position. Notice that the plate is not welded but secured by rivets and bolts, as the numerous drilled holes indicate.

Right, bottom: The foreship from starboard amidships. The battle-mast has been fitted but is still cluttered with staging. On the upper deck abaft the battle-mast are ventilation shafts. Construction of the bridge superstructure is proceeding, and the 7m rangefinder of the forward command post has been installed on the roof of the bridge porch. 'A' turret is complete and trained to port.

Left: A stern view of *Deutschland* nearing completion. The quarterdeck lacks only the two banks of torpedo tubes, the rotating bases for which are visible. 'B' turret is trained to starboard, probably for testing purposes. Staging is still present around the battle-mast and funnel. Notice the armoured window blinds on the rear bulkhead of the forecastle deck. Both propeller guards have been extended.

Above: A retouched photograph showing *Deutschland* during early engine trials. Even at that time there was a concerted effort to ensure that her machinery performance remained a secret. The rangefinder at the foretop is an artist's impression. The fire control system was not installed until the final stages of completion at Wilhelmshaven.

Right: *Deutschland* completing alongside the Wilhelmshaven Navy Yard fitting-out quay shortly before commissioning. To starboard of the ship is the canal leading into the launching basin. All gunnery direction systems save that of the Flak have been installed.

Above: *Deutschland* was commissioned on 1 April 1933. The ship's permanent company, 474 men, embarked en masse from the adjacent light cruiser *Emden*, which was due to refit. The Press was well represented for the occasion.

Below: Shortly before the commissioning ceremony, the ship's company take up allocated positions on deck and report by division. Notice the bank of torpedo tubes aft.

Above: The commander delivers his commissioning address to the ship's company.
Below: 'Hoist ensign and pennant!' To the strains of the *Flaggenmarsch* and the German National Anthem, *Deutsch-* *land* is commissioned into the Reichsmarine. Numerous photographers line the quayside. The quarterdeck torpedo tubes have been deleted from this photograph by the censor.

Above: The commissioned ship still at the fitting-out quay. Behind her either a 'K' class light cruiser or the predreadnought *Hessen*.

Left: *Deutschland*'s first commander, Kapitän zur See Hermann von Fischel (April 1933–September 1935).

Right, upper: *Deutschland* alongside at the Wilhelmshaven Navy Yard. To the left is the Langer Heinrich floating crane, and moored at the quay is the battleship *Hessen*. This photograph was taken from the swing-bridge connecting the peninsula to the harbour.

Right, lower: *Deutschland* at a mooring buoy in the Kielder Förde during the winter of 1933/34. The quarterdeck sentry wears a look-out's greatcoat and the blue cap cover usual for the season. Kitchen waste has probably just been thrown overboard – hence the gull activity.

Left: Two aerial photographs taken on 1 June 1933 showing *Deutschland* in one of the two chambers of Lock III at Wilhelmshaven Navy Yard. The upper view shows the starboard side of the ship. Beyond her is Lock II with its turning basin; the latter was the original lock, renumbered Lock II in the late 1880s following the building of the second lock. The lower photograph shows the ship from the other side. Adjacent to the lock is the so-called 'Woodman's Hollow Basin', with numerous gunnery targets plus harbour and shipyard craft. At the right there is a bathing facility. In the waterway an old *Deutschland* class battleship, either *Schlesien* or *Schleswig-Holstein*, is moored at the 'Alaska' anchorage.

Above right: From 10 to 14 April 1934 *Deutschland* made an unpublicised voyage to Norwegian waters with the Reich Chancellor, Reich War Minister, the C-in-Cs of Army and Navy and

other leading dignitaries aboard. Seen here on the bridge extension are (from left) Kapitän zur See Guse, C-in-C Fleet Division at Naval Command; Korvettenkapitän von Friedeburg, Naval ADC to the Reich War Minister; Reich War Minister Generaloberst von Blomberg; with his back to the camera Kapitän zur See von Fischel,

Deutschland's commander; Adolf Hitler; and Hitler's personal ADC, SA-Obergruppenführer Brückner.

Below: The cruise through the Nor-wegian fjords: approaching a village tucked between the shoreline and the foot of snow-capped mountains, as seen from the bridge overlooking the forecastle.

Left: Alongside the funnel, starboard side, can be seen the post of the loading derrick, to which two searchlight platforms have been added. According to the plans, these were unshipped later and replaced by an 8.8cm Flak twin. The view is astern from the bridge. Only a few years later Norway would become the haunt – and hide-out – of the German surface fleet.

Below: A broader perspective of the preceding view, with both starboard and port derrick posts. Around the funnel cap is the original array of aerial outriggers modified in a later refit.

Right, top: Many fjords are narrow and often appear unnegotiable on account of the precipitous mountains either side. Here a number of crew members take the opportunity for some photography.

Right, centre: Another view looking ahead from the bridge.

Right, bottom: Crewmen on the platform of the main gunnery direction centre at the foretop. Immediately above them is the armoured position itself, with viewing slits, and above that the 10.5cm rangefinder. The platform was later modified.

Left, upper: Navy Chief of Staff Admiral Raeder with *Deutschland*'s commander standing in front of one of the 15cm medium guns. Aboard all larger Kriegsmarine units the main guns, and often the individual gun batteries of the secondary armament, were given names in the naval tradition or of famous personalities. The two medium batteries aboard *Deutschland* were known as 'Tirpitz' and 'Köster'. Both men bore the rank of Grossadmiral: Tirpitz was State Secretary of the Admiralty and effectively the creator of the Imperial battle fleet from 1898 onwards; Karl von Köster was a German naval tactician of the pre-First World War era.

Left, lower: *Deutschland* hands enjoy the landscape from staging at the foot of the 10.5cm rangefinder in the area of the aft command centre.

Right, upper: A snowy mountain range lies abeam to port. In the davits a 10-oared cutter has been swung out ready for lowering – a normal measure to facilitate its immediate use in an emergency.

Right, lower: *Deutschland*'s crew parade on deck on arrival in Old Hamburg for the ship's official visit to the city between 28 May and 1 June 1934. Partially concealed by her smoke, and to the far left, are the pre-dreadnoughts *Schlesien* and *Schleswig-Holstein* respectively.

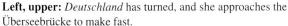

Left, upper: *Deutschland* has turned, and she approaches the Überseebrücke to make fast.

Left, lower: As always on such occasions, the public comes aboard. The crowds wander through the authorised open areas of the ship and plague the crew with questions. The star on the upper sleeve of the white blouse indicates an Ordinary Seaman: the other three crewmen are NCOs (navy blouse, white trousers).

Above left: One of the purposes of the Fleet visit was to commemorate the anniversary of the Battle of Jutland on 31 May. In this photograph Admiral Förster, C-in-C of the Navy, delivers his speech to ships' crews and other delegates.

Above right: A march past concludes the ceremony.

Right: A view of *Deutschland* from above the stem while made fast at Hamburg. An admiral's pennant flutters at the foretop and both bridge wings are fully extended. Note the modification to the foretop platform railing, the Flak direction installation below the centre searchlight and, a little lower on either side of the ladder, two further SL 2 Flak control units installed but not yet operational. To starboard of 'A' turret an honour guard, including a drummer, is being instructed in the 'Present arms' drill. Normally all officers were accorded 'Side', and the commander 'Front and side', on the bosun's pipe. According to status, VIPs and certain other shipboard guests boarding by the jack-ladder were entitled to receive on their arrival and departure a ceremonial on the pipe and a 'Present arms' from an honour guard with horn and drum.

Above: Shipboard routine and training. A bosun's mate (indicated by the foul-anchor patch on the upper sleeve) pipes 'Side'. On board ship, routine orders were given on the bosun's pipe. Each order had its individual sequence of shrills and an experienced seaman knew in advance what order would follow next. The two shoulder stripes denote No 2 port watch. The badge on the lower arm is that of a Flak Gun Captain (Geschützführer II); this was redesignated Gun Captain II (Light Flak) in 1940. The signals (right) are:

(1) 'Vergatterung!': 'Reminder of your duties!'
(2) 'Stillgestanden! Front nach Steuerbord': 'At attention, facing to starboard!'
(3) 'Stillgestanden! Front nach Backbord': 'At attention facing to port!'
(4) 'Flaggenparade!': 'Parade to the flag!'
(5) 'Locken zum Zapfenstreich!': 'Prepare to observe curfew!'
(6) 'Zapfenstreich!': 'Curfew!'
(7) 'Wecken!': 'Reveille!'
(8) 'Klar Schiff zum Gefecht!': 'Clear ship for battle!'

Above left: 'Ordinary Seaman Longsplice' – a home-made dummy for 'Man overboard' exercises.

Above right: Work involving all hands. Numerous members of the ship's company are seen engaged in running out lines either at the beginning or end of a manoeuvre – probably a towing exercise with another vessel. The off-duty watches would be called out by whistle for manoeuvres and exercises of this kind.

Below: Two photographs showing the Smadding ('Smarting') with his men clearing the anchor. Usually a time-served Warrant Officer, he was the Number One Boatswain to be found on every ship and boat supervising activities such as this.

Left: Quarterdeck seamen unkink a hawser for coiling aboard *Deutschland*.

Left: The daily grind aboard ship also included maintenance of the funnel mantle. The hot exhaust gases quickly gave the paintwork a burned look. Note the wind deflectors.

Left: Writers in one of the various administration offices.

Right: In fine weather the laundry – including the hammock as well as the sheets – was hung out to dry on the upper deck.

Right: Upkeep of clothing on an engineering deck. An Oberheizer (Senior Stoker; the rank was redesignated Machinist NCO in 1939) irons the collar of a naval blouse while others are occupied with make-and-mend.

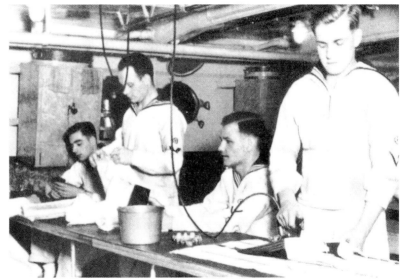

Right: The repetitive activity of cleaning ship. Here crewmen in cheerful mood give the wooden surface of the upper deck the necessary clean and shine with a broom. Aboard sail training ships and certain other vessels this task was taken to extremes, and sea cadets were required to kneel and scrub the deck with the 'prayer book' (a large pumice stone). This gave the wood an extra brightness.

Left: The Backschafter, or mess-table runner. In his right hand he carries the food pail, in his left its lid containing a net of potatoes. Every mess table had its Backschafter, who was normally appointed acording to a weekly rota. The duty involved collecting the rations for his mess-table (eight to ten men), supplying the cutlery and distributing the food – and washing up afterwards. Potato peeling was worked into shipboard routine: the number of potatoes peeled by the Backschafter dictated the weight apportioned to his table. This rating is a member of No 2 starboard watch.

Above: Backschafters form a queue to collect rations from the galley.

Below left: Mealtime on a seaman's mess deck. Knife, fork and plate indicates a 'full whack' (potatoes with vegetables, meat and gravy); a 'half-whack' was stew served in a bowl. Some obviously like it . . .

Below right: . . . others not so much. Using the ship's rail for support, a seaman 'feeds the fishes'. It could be some time before a man new to the sea finally conquered seasickness.

Above: Sport – on board or ashore – was highly favoured by the Navy. During the long periods of idleness during a voyage equipment would be set up on the upper deck, these four photographs showing vaulting, diving through the lifebelt, exercises on the horizontal bar and press-ups. The programme would always be full of variety.

Below left: Off-duty on the stokers' deck, playing cards, playing chess or doing nothing as the mood takes them. The chess player (right) has a patch in the design of a three-bladed propeller on the sleeve of his blouse below the service grade chevron. This indicates that he has passed Motor Course III.

Below right: An accommodation deck for Seaman Branch NCOs, where two decent games of skat seem to be in progress.

Top left: At Christmas, those remaining aboard – not all could have leave – celebrated in common irrespective of rank.

Top right: Sleeping quarters aboard *Deutschland*. Only warrant officers and above were entitled to a cabin and bunk; all other ranks, including midshipmen, had hammocks, which offered the advantage of comfort and stability in heavy seas.

Above left: A midday rest period in one of the seamen's decks. Some doze stretched along a bench, others have made use of netting as a hammock. The shipboard mascot, the brown bear Hokko, was always in evidence.

Above right: 'Smacking the hams' was said to be a much-loved shipboard activity(!).

Left: Free time on the upper deck. Most take the sun, but a boxing match attracts a number of interested spectators.

Right: Senior ratings watch a stage in the construction of a model of *Deutschland*. At the head of the table is an NCO wearing a collar and tie. He has a single star on his shoulder straps, which indicates the career path of a boatswain. Although these NCOs carried a ceremonial dagger and outwardly resembled warrant officers, they were senior grade petty officers eligible for promotion on account of time served but not qualified by examination. They dined in the warrant officers' mess but were lodged with the petty officers.

Below: The high point of every voyage below the Equator was the ceremony for all officers and men 'Crossing the Line' for the first time. The South America cruise to test diesel endurance was the only occasion when *Deutschland* left the northern hemisphere.

Left: An engineer officer and other watch personnel at the so-called 'cylinder station' in one of the motor rooms.

Left: A stoker attends one of the two auxiliary boilers.

Left: The ship was equipped with a number of workshops. This is the carpenters' . . .

Right: . . . and here a mechanic at a lathe in the gunnery workshop is busy with a replacement part.

Right and below right: Particularly in peacetime, it was naval routine – more often than not at weekends – to hold a commander's inspection. The entire ship's company would fall in by division and each crewman would be subjected to scrutiny in some way. On this occasion there is a cap inspection, in which the white man-o'-war cover and brim would have to be in an impeccable condition, with the name tally properly tied and the crown raised at the front by a thin metal prong in the prescribed manner.

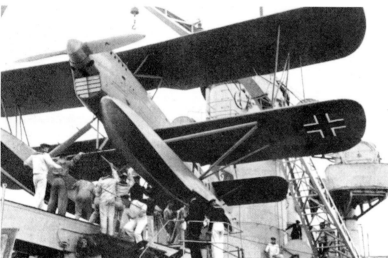

Left, top: *Deutschland* at Kiel opposite the Blücherbrücke, where the sail training ship *Gorch Fock* has made fast. Forward of the latter is the old signal station, with which *Deutschland* appears to be in contact – note the signaller perched on the railings of the signal bridge wing. On the foredeck are the powerful starboard anchor capstan and chain.

Left, centre: Clearing down the shipboard aircraft. The Heinkel 60 was the initial issue to all German heavy ships. The type was developed in 1931–32 as a shipboard reconnaissance two-seat biplane with an open cockpit and floats, suitable for catapult launching. The prototype appeared in August 1932. The aircraft had good flight characteristics and was nimble. However, the pilot had a poor view, and despite the armament of a fixed MG 17 and a flexible MG 15 the He 60 was very vulnerable. The aircraft's BMW Type VI U 6.0 Z engine produced 660hp (Daimler Benz developed their DM 600 engine with an output of 1,000hp for a speed of 290kph but this was never fitted). All-up weight was 3,600kg, top speed 235kph, fuel capacity 470 litres and range 640km.

Left, bottom: A catapult launch for *Deutschland*'s He 60.

Right, upper: *Deutschland* entering Lock III at Wilhelmshaven on 3 July 1934. A lengthy absence is in prospect – probably the visit to Scotland and Sweden followed by the autumn fleet manoeuvres. The propeller guards are extended and the crew has gathered on the upper deck for the departure.

Right, lower: *Deutschland* entering the Scottish port of Leith for a visit in August 1934.

Left: The ship was often called upon to prove her sea-keeping qualities. This view from the bridge shows the force with which oncoming seas swept the foredeck. On the roof of 'A' turret is the aircraft recognition signal from Imperial Navy times, a white ring on a dark background.

Below: Seas on the port quarter during a Biscay storm. These great rolling masses rose substantially higher than in German home waters.

Above: The aftermath of gunnery practice for the main armament: 'A' turret is at rest and numerous shell cases are strewn around the upper deck. The railing stanchions were lowered whenever the guns were in action.

Below left: Material was precious: on the completion of each gunnery exercise the shell cases were collected up and carefully stowed away.

Below right: Each exercise was followed by gun cleaning. The 28cm main barrels needed a large squad to handle this relatively heavy work.

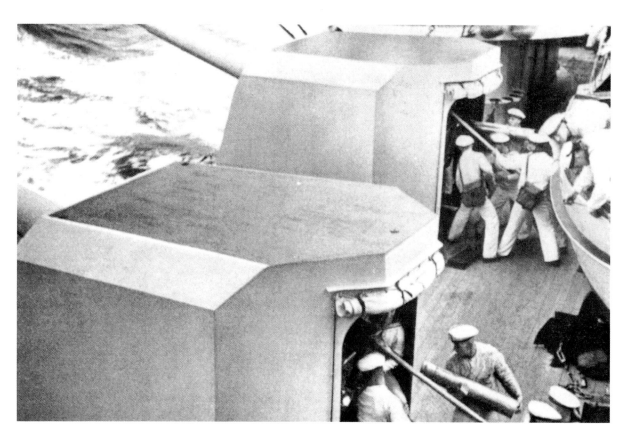

Left, upper: Maximum effort from the secondary armament at practice. Note the open area at the rear of the armoured gunhouses.

Left, lower: A 15cm gunhouse as seen from the bridge.

Above: Laying a smoke screen. The smoke-making apparatus was at the stern. In use it ejected thick billows of white smoke which spread relatively quickly to form a thick and visually impenetrable wall.

Below: An aerial view of *Deutschland*. The belt armour is clearly visible, as is, just below it, the top of the anti-torpedo bulge. The horizontal post on the ship's side is the forward mooring boom in the stowed position. Between the battle-mast and funnel is the revolving aircraft catapult, and to the port side of the funnel the lattice crane. Note the four starboard 15cm gunhouses, and also the twin-barrelled 8.8cm HA/LA guns located abreast the funnel.

Above: *Deutschland* from her port quarter. The propeller guard has been extended and a rope ladder lowered beside the stern anchor for informal use of the ship's boats. At the foot of the jack-ladder amidships a communications launch is being boarded while the commander's pinnace waits alongside. Note the altered configuration of the aerial yards on the funnel, the newly installed mainmast and the new, short pole mast atop the rangefinder of the aft control centre.

Below: *Deutschland* leaving Kieler Förde.

Above: People's Navy Week at Kiel, May–June 1936, during which period the naval memorial at Laboe was dedicated in the presence of Hitler. He took the salute aboard *Grille* at the Naval Review of 29 May, and here *Deutschland*'s crew parades the length of the deck to starboard on passing the State yacht.

Below left: A view of *Deutschland* looking aft from the foretop gallery. Sister-ship *Admiral Scheer* is astern.

Below right: Following the outbreak of the Spanish Civil War in 1936, *Deutschland* formed part of the international task force exercising naval control over Spain's territorial waters. For identification purposes the main turrets were painted in stripes of the national colours. Days of constant operations were followed by long peaceful interludes in which sunbathing on the forecastle deck was popular.

Above: *Deutschland* at Alicante early in the Civil War. The smoke indicates fighting in the city.

Below: A meeting between sister-ships in a Spanish port: *Admiral Scheer* seen from *Deutschland*'s forecastle.

Right: The incident at Ibiza in the early evening of 29 May 1937. An amateur photographer took this exposure of *Deutschland*, hit and on fire, immediately after the attack by Republican aircraft. Two 50kg bombs were responsible for all the damage in the succeeding photographs. The question whether *Deutschland* had her AA armament manned at the time has never been answered.

Opposite page: A view of the forecastle deck, 'A' turret clearly showing the national markings. All crew members of this turret were either killed or wounded. The pressure from the explosion blew off a door to the battle-mast and converted it into a chimney, smoke from the fire passing upwards through the tower and out at foretop level.

Right: Pumps laid out ready, a damage control party equipped with gas masks begins the firefighting operation on the port side of the ship.

Below left: The impact site of the first bomb hit: the starboard upper deck alongside the bridge.

Below right and bottom: The effects of the hit at Frame 116. These three exposures show the extent of the devastation as crewmen begin the work of clearing the damage.

Above left: Starboard III 15cm gunhouse was also damaged.
Above right: Below the impact site of the first bomb.
Below: Only the steel framework of the He 60 shipboard aircraft survived.

Left: The remains of the 15cm ready ammunition locker near the Senior NCO's mess. One shell was retrieved undamaged.

Below: *Deutschland* on arrival at Gibraltar, her crew assembled by division for work allocation. Astern, right, is a flotilla of British destroyers at their moorings.

Opposite page: Burial of *Deutschland*'s dead at Gibraltar with full military honours. Many of the Rock's population lined the processional route. On Hitler's orders the remains were exhumed on the night of 11 June 1937 and brought aboard *Deutschland* in the harbour at Gibraltar. This was not publicised, and only aboard ship was there any ceremonial.

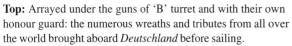

Top: Arrayed under the guns of 'B' turret and with their own honour guard: the numerous wreaths and tributes from all over the world brought aboard *Deutschland* before sailing.

Above: The return to Germany. On the quarterdeck the dead of Ibiza lie in state. Two honour guards have been mounted, side-arms drawn, arms crossed.

Right: The German battle ensign is flown at half mast from the staff atop the after command centre.

Above: *Deutschland* at anchor on 15 June 1937 in Schilling Roads for cosmetic repairs before entering Wilhelmshaven.
Below: After the ship made fast alongside the Gazelle-Brücke in the main harbour, *Deutschland*'s dead were brought ashore at nightfall and the cortège proceeded to the Wilhelmshaven military cemetery in a torchlit procession through the silent, crowded streets of the city.

Top: The arrival at Wilhelmshaven military cemetery of high-ranking personalities, 17 June 1937. Proceeding past an honour guard are Konteradmiral von Nordeck (Senior Shipyard Manager, saluting), Admiral Carls (Fleet C-in-C), Admiral Schultze (Commanding Admiral, Naval Station North Sea) and between these latter two *Deutschland*'s commander, Kapitän zur See Fanger. The tall figure concealed immediately behind Hitler is Reich War Minister Generalfeldmarschall von Blomberg. To his left is Generaladmiral Raeder.

Above: Also paying their final respects on behalf of the Spanish Nationalist Government are, from left, flanked by a Kriegsmarine liaison officer, the Spanish Ambassador with escort and (in uniform) the Military Attaché.

Right: The captain takes his leave of his dead crewmen.

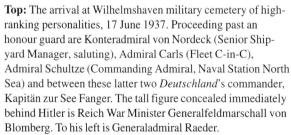

Top: The C-in-C of the Army, Generaloberst von Fritsch, who had a special attachment to *Deutschland*, pays his last respects. Behind him are his ADC and Kapitän zur See Fanger.
Above: In connection with the funeral the ship's company paraded on the quarterdeck to receive an address from Hitler. Behind the latter are (from left) Carls, von Blomberg and Raeder. In the background is a square hulk, the remains of the former pre-dreadnought battleship *Preussen*.
Right: Kapitän zur See Fanger took his leave as *Deutschland*'s commander on 30 September 1937. Here the crew parade 'front to port' as the captain treads the platform of the accommodation ladder and reports his departure to the Officer of the Watch. Saluting, at left, is the First Officer; in white blouses are members of the ladder honour party.

Above: The bomb damage was quickly repaired and *Deutschland*, seen here at the Wilhelmshaven fitting-out quay with *Admiral Scheer* nearby, soon reported fully operational. Notice the new shipboard cranes and raked funnel cap.

Below: A map showing the route of the fifth Spanish cruise, which got under way soon after the completion of repairs.

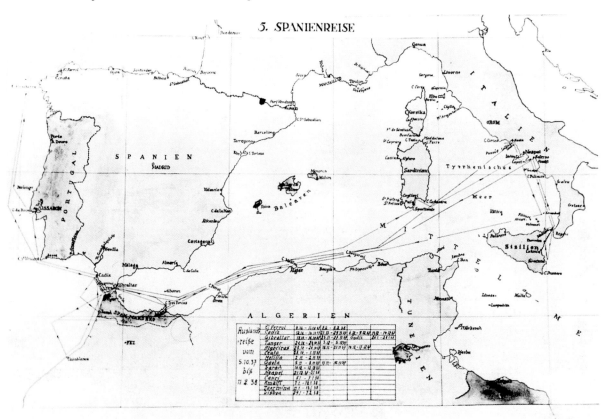

Left: Captain's Parade on the quarterdeck in Mediterranean waters.

Below: After the Ibiza disaster all anti-aircraft weapons were manned constantly, with gun crews closed up whenever the ship was near Spanish waters. Beyond the 15cm gunhouses an 8.8cm twin mounting rakes the skies. In the foreground, targeting equipment is also manned.

Above: Use was made of the short time in home waters and passages through the Eastern Atlantic to and from Spanish operations for gunnery practice. This photograph shows 'B' turret firing salvos. Notice the closed armoured shutters over the windows on the rear face of the superstructure and the top of one of the banks of torpedo tubes.

Left: 'A' turret fires a salvo ahead. The two main 28cm turrets were named: 'A' turret was dubbed 'Hitler' and decorated with the Party insignia, and 'B' turret was named 'Hindenburg' and bore his coat of arms. In September 1939 all external decorations, including even the eagle and swastika at the stern and the national shield at the bow, were removed from the ship for security reasons; only the names remained. When *Deutschland* was renamed *Lützow* in November 1939 the turret names became an embarrassment: whereas Hitler and Hindenburg were German national leaders, the ship itself bore only the name of a Freikorps leader of the Napoleonic Wars.

Above: 'B' turret in action again.
Right, upper: The secondary armament during gunnery practice at night.
Right, lower: Weather conditions at sea are always variable. Here the bows plough deeply into the oncoming waves. The great pile of water would be shrugged sternwards to wash round 'A' turret – if not further.

Above: Over Christmas 1937 and the New Year *Deutschland* was at Naples, where she is seen here moored stern to quay in the Mediterranean custom. To her port are four *Albatros* class torpedo-boats and in the background the snow-topped peak of Vesuvius.

Below: On the occasion of the launching of the heavy cruiser *Prinz Eugen* at Kiel on 22 August 1938, a Naval Review was held off the Kieler Förde. Here the three units of the *Deutschland* class – *Admiral Graf Spee* bringing up the rear – re-enter the Förde in line ahead at the conclusion of the proceedings. At *Deutschland*'s foretop is the national flag of Hungary.

Right, upper: The war clouds gather. After the 'Spanish adventure' the German warships returned to home stations. Here *Deutschland* heads for Germany a few months before the outbreak of the European War.

Right, lower: Now reclassified as a heavy cruiser, the former Panzerschiff *Deutschland* is shown here in the winter of 1939/ 40, guns, decks and superstructure glittering with a mantle of ice which her crew members are at pains to remove in an effort to keep the ship at operational readiness while at anchor.

Above: Renamed *Lützow*, the cruiser was assigned to Warship Group 5 with the objective of landing occupation troops at Oslo during 'Weserübung', the invasion of Denmark and Norway. This involved passing through the hazardous Dröbak Narrows in full view of well-concealed Norwegian shore batteries, and the flagship, the *Hipper* class heavy cruiser *Blücher*, was duly sunk. As the second ship in line, *Lützow* was also soon damaged, with four dead, and the commander used his discretion. Returning to Germany, the ship unwisely risked the voyage alone through submarine-infested waters and met with disaster off Skagen when torpedoed in the stern by a British submarine in the early hours of 11 April 1940.

The German ship wallowed rudderless and propellerless for hours before the first flotilla of escort vessels arrived. In this photograph, which shows the extent of her predicament, several minesweepers provide protection.

Below: The cruiser seen from off the port beam. Her stern has been almost snapped off abaft the rear of the forecastle deck and is fully submerged save for the top of the torpedo tube sets breaking surface. Alongside a UJ-boat gives close anti-submarine escort. Note the Arado 196 floatplane on the catapult. This type replaced the Heinkel 60 at the outbreak of war.

Above: Only 7nm off Skagen and drifting inshore at 2kt, the stricken cruiser waits for tugs to arrive.
Below: *Lützow* in the shipyard at Kiel, her severed after section clearly visible. It was discovered on inspection that only the two propeller shafts had been keeping the stern attached to the ship. The two banks of torpedo tubes have already been unshipped.

Left: Three photographs of *Lützow* in drydock. Top and centre: the damage inflicted to the stern and the starboard shaft. Both propellers sheared off when the torpedo struck. Bottom: the hull above and below the waterline to port, showing the failure of the welding in the impact area. The keel strakes also received serious damage.

Right, top: *Lützow* in early 1941 following her repairs. In this photograph the cruiser is at Kieler Förde on 24 March that year, with a newly installed FuMO radar aerial and observation centre at the foretop.

Right, centre: The cruiser moored offshore at Kiel and wearing the 1941 Baltic camouflage pattern.

Right, bottom: This starboard view, for comparison, shows the similarity of the camouflage scheme on either side of the ship.

Above: *Lützow* in Kieler Förde in March or early April 1941.
Below: *Lützow* slow ahead, seen entering the port of
Gotenhafen on 12 April 1941 to work up for Operation
'Sommerreise'. Behind her stern is the great bulk of *Bismarck*,
45 days before the battleship's disastrous end. SKL did not
accept the latter as history's verdict on the use of regular
warships as commerce raiders, and *Lützow* duly sailed for the
Indian Ocean via Trondheim on 12 June. She got as far as
Egersund before a British torpedo-aircraft put an end to the
adventure.

Above: At Gotenhafen in 1942. In contrast to the previous year, the Baltic paint scheme is now dark grey overall. In the background between the two white masts (left) are the tower, funnel and mainmast of the battlecruiser *Scharnhorst*, sent to Norway in 1943 and lost off the North Cape on Boxing Day in action against a superior British naval force. Nearest the camera is one of the passenger liners laid up at Gotenhafen as accommodation ships: the white livery suggests a hospital ship – by the look of her masts, possibly *Hansa*.

Below: *Lützow* leaving Gotenhafen some time in 1942. At the quay on the far side of the harbour basin are, from left, the ice-breaker *Castor*, the pre-dreadnought battleship *Schlesien* and the light cruiser *Emden*.

Left, upper: An aerial view of *Lützow* at Norway within a screen of anti-torpedo nets. Amidships, her floatplane manoeuvres alongside. She has a few boats in the water, for which the port accommodation ladder has been lowered for access.

Left, lower: *Lützow* during the closing operations in the East, 1945: the stern as seen from the funnel platform.

Below: The naval base at Swinemünde in 1944, as seen from an Allied reconnaissance aircraft. The large curved breakwater is the Eichstaden. Alongside are (1) *Lützow* and (2) *Admiral Scheer* and the stern of the light cruiser *Emden*; ship (3) is the light cruiser *Köln*.

Left: A view over the bow from the bridge, during operations in the East. Note the 2cm Flak gun under a tarpaulin abaft the break-water. 'A' turret is trained to port.

Below: *Lützow* in late 1944, with FuMO and FuMB radar antennas at the foretop.

Above: *Lützow* at speed in the Baltic in late 1944. The FuMB equipment is no longer fitted.

Below: The wreck of *Lützow* photographed at Swinemünde shortly after the capitulation. Having expended her remaining ammunition to bombard Soviet forces from mid-April, the cruiser was abandoned, but she survived a scuttling attempt by explosives on 3/4 May 1945. Her subsequent whereabouts are unknown.

Panzerschiff *Admiral Scheer*

Origin of the Name

Reinhard Scheer (born in Obernkirchen on 30 September 1863, died at Marktredwitz on 26 November 1928) entered the Imperial Navy as a cadet on 22 April 1879 and was commissioned on 16 November 1882. He attained Flag rank as Konteradmiral Scheer on 27 January 1910 and as Vizeadmiral commanded the High Seas Fleet at Jutland on 31 May 1916. The late Vizeadmiral Ruge recorded: 'From taking over the High Seas Fleet, Scheer was bent on deploying it operationally and if possible bringing the British Grand Fleet to battle. When this great clash occurred off Jutland, the Royal Navy suffered much heavier losses than the German Fleet. Scheer proved himself a skilled tactician when by the use of numerous course changes he avoided a threatening closing manoeuvre which threw the British battle line into confusion.' Jutland was a tactical German victory, but the Fleet now retired to its Baltic and North Sea hide-outs for the remainder of the war and, apart from occasional forays, did nothing more.

Scheer's reputation had soared after Jutland and he made the convincing argument to the Kaiser and naval planners that a second battle might not have such a favourable outcome as the first. Therefore, he argued strongly for unrestricted U-boat warfare. From August 1918, as Chief of the Admiral Staff and head of the Seekriegsleitung, he negotiated with industry the 'Scheer Programme', which aimed at the monthly production of 36 new U-boats. However, by then it was too late. He firmly opposed, on strategic grounds, a plan to seek a last decisive encounter with the Grand Fleet, although it was probably impracticable in any case because of the mutinies and disaffection aboard the big ships at that late stage of the war.

He retired as a full Admiral on 17 December 1918. His decorations include the Ordre Pour le Mérite and Oak Leaves, awarded on 5 June 1916 and 1 February 1918 respectively.

Ship's Career

The building contract for *Admiral Scheer* was placed with the Marine Werft, Wilhelmshaven, as Panzerschiff 'B' ('Replacement *Lothringen*'), Builder's Number 123. The first

Above: Admiral Reinhard Scheer, commanding officer of the German High Seas Fleet at the Battle of Jutland, photographed shortly before his retirement in December 1918.

keel elements were laid on 25 June 1931 but construction was dragged out on account of the economic situation and to retain over as long a period as possible the yard's qualified craftsmen then under threat of redundancy.

The hull was launched on 1 April 1933 a few hours after the commissioning of *Deutschland* at Kiel. Before numerous VIPs and former Imperial Navy officers, including Admirals Trotha and Behncke, the baptismal speech was delivered by Admiral Raeder and the naming ceremony performed by Frau Marianne Besserer, daughter of the late Admiral Scheer.

The initial shipyard trials took place on 1 October 1934. The ship was commissioned on 12 November 1934, her permanent company being transferred in from the old pre-dreadnought *Hessen* decommissioning the same day. Hard drill and exercises followed prior to the 'Fitness for Sea' inspection carried out by C-in-C Battleships (BdL) on 13 December.

1935

In March the ship forced a way through heavy ice for a visit to the Baltic city of Königsberg. After completion of the obligatory trials programme on 18 April, the Panzerschiff was attached to the BdL Squadron and further weeks of working-up ensued. The Fleet C-in-C, Admiral Förster, was aboard *Admiral Scheer* for the Jutland Remembrance Day ceremonies between 30 May and 2 June at Stettin alongside the sail training ship *Gorch Fock*. On Ascension Day alone about 10,000 people visited the ship, including the aged former Feldmarschall von Mackensen. In the city the Skagerrakplatz was dedicated in the presence of the crew and two thoroughfares were named Graf Spee-Strasse and Admiral Scheer-Strasse. The record for visitors to the ship was set during People's Navy Week at Kiel when 38,000 persons were counted as boarding during a four-day period. These included Adolf Hitler, Rudolf Hess and Admiral Raeder.

Königsberg was visited for a second time in July. *Admiral Scheer*, which was the largest ship ever to have visited the city, grounded lightly in the Pillau–Königsberg Canal but the bottom was sandy and no damage was reported. On 30 August and 1 September, when the ship called at Danzig, a crowd of 100,000 onlookers cheered her arrival from the shore and another 40,000 waited in the old Markt to greet the crew.

Between 19 October and 9 November the ship carried out the usual programme of gunnery exercises in Atlantic waters, calling at Madeira. In the North Sea on the return, hurricane force winds were encountered. Whilst running to render assistance to a French steamer in distress on the Amrum Bank, the bow was stove in by heavy seas off Heligoland. Carpenters shored up the damaged section and *Admiral Scheer* headed for Cuxhaven stern-first to ride out the storm.

1936

During May *Admiral Scheer* was at Kiel. On the 29th she took part in the Naval Review in front of Hitler and on the 31st was one of the honour formation units for the dedication of the naval memorial at Laboe.

On 6 June she was the flagship of Admiral Förster for a round voyage of the British Isles via the Channel, Irish Sea and Skagen to Kiel in company with her sister-ship *Deutschland*. *Admiral Scheer* was in Swedish waters from 23 to 29 June, King Gustav V visiting the ship in Stockholm. On returning to Kiel on 2 July, Admiral Förster transferred his flag to *Admiral Graf Spee*. *Admiral Scheer* anchored in the roadstead at Heligoland on 21 July preparatory to commencing gunnery and AA exercises but was recalled abruptly to Wilhelmshaven on the 23rd, where she arrived at 1700 and dropped anchor near *Deutschland*. Live ammunition was shipped aboard and the vessel was fitted out for a long operation in foreign waters. At 2100 Kapitän zur See Wilhelm Marschall had the ship's company assemble for an address in which the mission and its objective were made known. On 24 July the BdL, Konteradmiral Carls, hoisted his pennant in *Deutschland*'s yard and the two Panzerschiffe sailed at once. On the 26 *Admiral Scheer* rounded Cape Finisterre on detachment to the Mediterranean while *Deutschland* remained in the Bay of Biscay. After passing through the Strait of Gibraltar on the 27th, she made a six-hour call at Malaga the same day, sailing at 1700 for Barcelona, where she arrived at 1400 on the 28th.

Civil war had broken out in Spain and the German warships had the task of removing German citizens from the danger area, although assistance was never refused to other nationals requesting it. During August *Admiral Scheer* also visited Almeria (3rd) and Tarragona (4th). She was at Gibraltar from 26 to 27 August and sailed to rendezvous with *Deutschland* and the torpedo-boats *Luchs* and *Leopard* on the 28th for the homeward voyage. In order to increase the overall speed of the squadron, each Panzerschiff took a torpedo-boat in tow, but the hawsers parted continually and the idea was abandoned. After refuelling, the two smaller vessels continued under their own steam. Heavy fog quickly reduced the overall speed to 9kt for a period of eight hours, but the Strait of Dover was reached towards 1800 and *Admiral Scheer* entered the Kiel Canal at midday on 30 August to make fast at Kiel by nightfall. Most of the ship's company were given leave and replacements were embarked. Kapitän zur See Otto Ciliax became the new commander on 22 September.

The second Spanish tour of duty occupied the period from 2 October to 3 December (Wilhelmshaven–Kiel) with calls at numerous ports. Supervision within the framework of the International Naval Control Commission had begun to take effect. On her return to Kiel *Admiral Scheer* went into drydock.

1937

Admiral Scheer left Wilhelmshaven for her third Spanish tour (15 March to 7 April) and left Kiel for her fourth tour on 9 May. Calls were made at Nationalist-held ports. On 21 May, off Cartagena, Republican destroyers approached but turned sharply away when it was clear that the German ship was at readiness. The incident happened so quickly that it was not certain that there had been any hostile intent. On the 26th of the month, Republican destroyers were observed at sea exercising their gun crews. Upon the receipt of signals at 1600 that day, the command bridge was fully manned and, at full battle-readiness, the ship headed for Palma on course 350°. The commander informed the crew that an Italian warship had been attacked in the roadstead at Palma. A German warship had been in close proximity. From now on a war-watch status would be maintained. *Admiral Scheer* arrived off Ibiza at daybreak on the 27th and dropped anchor for a few hours.

Deutschland was expected on 29 May, but meanwhile *Admiral Scheer* resumed her patrol and was off Cartagena that evening when alarm bells gave notice of a fresh emergency. Battle stations were manned, the commander summoned all officers to the wardroom and the ship headed for the open sea at high speed. It was announced to the ship's company that *Deutschland* had sustained serious casualties and damage when bombed at anchor at Ibiza by Republican aircraft. The flags on *Admiral Scheer* were then flown at half-mast. Towards midnight she met the still-burning *Deutschland* and accompanied her sister-ship as far as Malaga before turning back to rendezvous with four torpedo-boats to await developments. On 30 May, while *Scheer* was refuelling off the Republican-held city of Alicante, Republican warships approached but withdrew swiftly when caught in the blinding glare of the German ship's searchlights.

During the early hours of Jutland Day, 31 May, *Admiral Scheer* doused all lights and ran down the coast in company with the four torpedo-boats. At 0400 the crew was notified of orders to bombard the Republican-held town of Almeria as a reprisal for the attack on *Deutschland*. With paravanes streamed and the four torpedo-boats *Seeadler*, *Albatros*, *Luchs* and *Leopard* on her flanks for security, *Admiral Scheer* manoeuvred to bear and at 0729 the main and secondary armament, plus 8.8cm Flak, were given permission to open a withering fire on the coastal batteries, the port and harbour installations and any shipping there. As she turned away, only a few coastal guns managed a reply.

While heading for the pre-arranged meeting point near Gibraltar with *Deutschland* and all remaining German Mediterranean units, *Admiral Scheer* flew the old Imperial War Flag at the foretop to commemorate Jutland Day. The squadron followed the southern shoreline before refuelling on 6 June and spending a few days at Tangier. The Panzerschiff was the flagship of Konteradmiral von Fischel, BdSP (Befehlshaber der Seestreitkräfte in Spanien, or C-in-C German Naval Forces in Spain) from 10 to 23 June, when control duties were resumed. *Deutschland* had been replaced by the light cruiser *Leipzig*, and after a brief meeting between the two Panzerschiffe near Gibraltar *Deutschland* headed for home while *Admiral Scheer* refuelled at Tangier and called at Gibraltar. The commander made an overdue gunnery inspection on 22 June before the German squadron headed back to Cartagena, where the individual units proceeded to their respective control areas. On 26 June *Admiral Scheer* was relieved by *Admiral Graf Spee* at Cadiz, and on 1 July she arrived at Wilhelmshaven.

Less than a month elapsed before the ship set out on 30 July for her next Spanish tour, as Fleet flagship of Admiral Carls, from 3 August also BdSP. He was relieved by Konteradmiral von Fischel for the period 8 September to 8 October. On 11 October the ship returned to Wilhelmshaven for an overhaul. There had been a significant turnover of personnel during the year, and on leaving the dockyard *Admiral Scheer* spent the remainder of the year in the Baltic for crew training.

1938

Training continued until February, when orders were received to undertake the sixth Spanish control mission (12 February to 14 March), as flagship of the BdSP from 16 February. The seventh and final tour lasted from 19 March (ex Wilhelmshaven) to 29 June. Upon the ship's return a comprehensive programme of fleet manoeuvres, gunnery exercises and battle training occupied the last six months of the year, broken only by a stay at Kiel for the Naval Review of 22 August on the occasion of the launching of the heavy cruiser *Prinz Eugen* in the presence of Hitler and the Hungarian regent Admiral von Horthy. Kapitän zur See Hans-Heinrich Wurmbach became *Admiral Scheer*'s third commander on 31 October 1938.

1939

In February *Admiral Scheer* was at Hamburg for the launch of the battleship *Bismarck* and in March, as flagship of the BdP Konteradmiral Marschall, the ship's former first commander, she formed part of the fleet squadron escorting Hitler to the Memel for the reincorporation of the old

German province into what had been termed the previous year the 'Greater German Reich'.

On 18 April the ship sailed for the Atlantic for exercises, visiting Portugal from the 22nd to the 27th of the month and returning to Wilhelmshaven on 3 May. The remaining months prior to the outbreak of hostilities with Britain and France on 3 September were devoted to crew training, working up and various tests and trials.

On 4 September the first sirens wailed over Frisia when three Whitley bombers of No 51 Squadron RAF overflew North Germany dropping leaflets. That same afternoon ten Bristol Blenheim bombers of Nos 107 and 110 Squadrons approached the Jade estuary with orders to attack any German warships found either in the Schilling roadstead or in harbour at Wilhelmshaven. The aircraft divided into two formations of five, No 110 Squadron attacking *Admiral Scheer*. One aircraft obtained three hits with 500lb bombs, all of which failed to explode and were jettisoned. Shipboard Flak accounted for one bomber. Four of the five Blenheims of the other group were shot down by Flak over Wilhelmshaven, one crashing into the deck of the light cruiser *Emden* which was manoeuvring in harbour, thus occasioning the first Kriegsmarine war dead of the new conflict. At Brunsbüttel, fourteen Wellington bombers from Nos 9 and 149 Squadrons RAF made an unsuccessful attack on the battlecruisers *Scharnhorst* and *Gneisenau* for the loss of two of their number at the hands of Bf 109s of *JG 77*.

Admiral Scheer spent the final quarter of the year crew training in the Baltic, where frequent diesel breakdowns dictated the advent of the planned and long overdue major overhaul – particularly for the engine plant –which eventually extended to the ship being rebuilt. On 31 October Kapitän zur See Theodor Krancke became the ship's fourth commander.

1940

The planned refit and major engine overhaul began at Wilhelmshaven on 1 February. During the lay-up, as acting Konteradmiral, Kapitän zur See Krancke was the naval representative attached to Special Staff Weserübung at OKW, and from 12 April to 16 June he held the office of Chief of Staff to Commanding Admiral, Norway.

Admiral Scheer emerged from the shipyard on 31 July with an altered appearance and reclassified officially as a heavy cruiser. From Frame 112 forward the stem had been modified better to combat breaking seas and the ship's length overall had been increased by 1.9m. The anchor cluses at the bow had been re-sited to reduce the ingress of water. The characteristic pagoda-like mast had been replaced by a tubular mast and the foretop had been re-modelled to accommodate FuMO 26 radar equipment. The funnel platform had been enlarged and a slightly raked funnel cap fitted. About 1.8m abaft the funnel a new mainmast had been erected with its support struts against the funnel. A degaussing system had been installed and the useless anti-roll device discarded.

On 31 July the heavy cruiser transferred to the Baltic port of Gotenhafen for intensive working-up. Minor engine problems were dealt with in collaboration with shipyard technicians at Danzig. The ship reported operational readiness relatively quickly, and on 23 October, during a crew muster, the commander announced the impending Atlantic commerce-raiding mission.

After passing through the Kiel Canal, *Admiral Scheer* sailed from Brunsbüttel for Stavanger on 27 October in company with her escorting oiler *Nordmark* and three torpedo-boats. In heavy weather on 31 October/1 November she broke out through the Denmark Strait.

The exceptionally successful voyage extended to the north of Madagascar in the Indian Ocean, and the cruiser proved able to elude all searching forces. Seventeen merchant vessels of 113,233brt fell victim, plus the armed merchant cruiser *Jervis Bay*. In the period between 23 October 1940 and 1 April 1941 the ship covered 46,419nm in 161 days, the diesels proving exceptionally reliable.

Admiral Scheer was replenished on a number of occasions during the cruise, principally by *Nordmark* but also from the requisitioned merchant tanker *Eurofeld*: on 18 November 1,327.9m³ diesel fuel, 14.5m³ lubricating oil, 42.4 tonnes provisions, 163.4 tonnes ammunition and one torpedo; on 14 December 1,142.2m³ diesel fuel, 27m³ lubricating oil, 55 tonnes provisions, 0.7 tonnes ammunition, 1.4 tonnes other goods; on 29 December 656.4m³ diesel fuel, 17.1m³ lubricating oil, 14.5 tonnes provisions and 4.4 tonnes other goods; on 7 January 247m³ diesel fuel; and on 5 January 524.6m³ diesel fuel, 33.5m³ lubricating oil, 57.1 tonnes provisions, three torpedoes and 6.4 tonnes ammunition.

The problem of ammunition resupply, particularly with regard to the weight of the 28cm shell, is highlighted by this record. In both world wars it was the Achilles' heel of German units in remote parts of the globe as events in the southern oceans bear witness – in 1914 (Graf von Spee's cruiser squadron) and in 1939 (the Panzerschiff *Admiral Graf Spee*).

There were meetings with other German warships engaged in commerce warfare in these latitudes – between

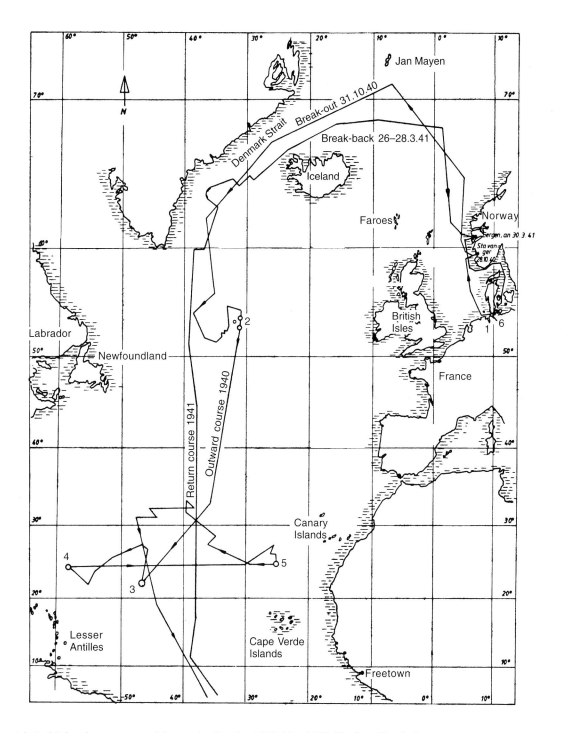

Above: *Admiral Scheer*'s commerce-raiding cruise,October 1940–May 1941, Northern Hemisphere
Key (all merchant sinkings British flag unless otherwise stated): (1) 27.10.40 sailed Brunsbüttel. (2) 5.11.40 sank *Mopan* (5,389brt), attacked convoy HX.4 and sank AMC *Jervis Bay* (14,164brt) after short engagement plus freighters *Maidan* (7,908brt), *Trewellard* (5,201brt), *Beaverford* (10,042brt), *Kanbane Head* (5,225brt) and *Fresno City* (4,955brt). (3) Replenishment from tanker *Eurofeld* 12.11.40 and oiler *Nordmark* 14.11.40. (4) 24.11.40 sank refrigerator ship *Port Hobart* (7,448brt). (5) 1.12.40 sank freighter *Tribesman* (6,242brt). (6) 1.4.40 arrived Kiel.

125

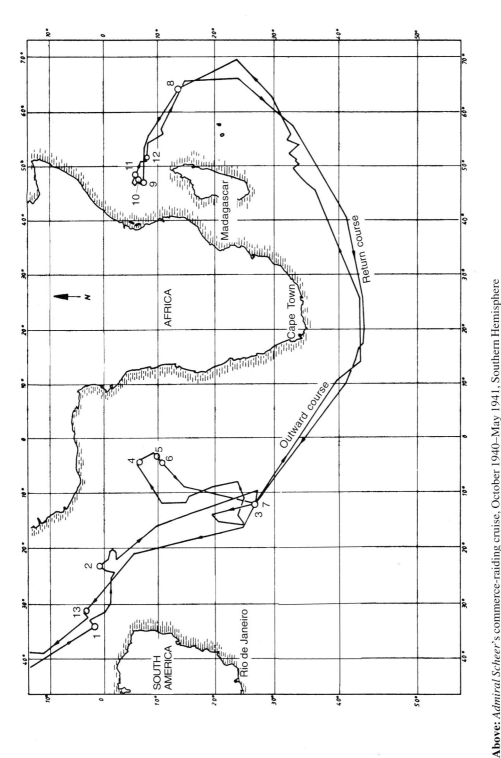

Above: *Admiral Scheer*'s commerce-raiding cruise, October 1940–May 1941, Southern Hemisphere
Key: (1) 14–15.12.40 replenished by naval oiler *Nordmark*. (2) 18.12.40 refrigerator ship *Duquesa* (8,561brt) captured and sent with prize crew to (3). (3) 25.12.40–5.1.41 rendezvous with *Nordmark*, *Eurofeld*, raider *Thor* and prize *Storstad*. (4) 18.1.41 captured tanker *Sandefjord* (10,000brt), ship under prize crew to (7) below. (5) 19.1.41 captured Dutch freighter *Barneveld* (5,200brt), ship scuttled 20.1.41. (6) 19.1.41 sank *Stanpark* (5,600brt). (7) 24–28.1.41 rendezvous with *Nordmark* and prize *Sandefjord*; 18.2.41 *Duquesa* scuttled by raider *Pinguin*. (8) 14–17.2.41 rendezvous with raider *Atlantis*, blockade-runner *Tannenfels* and prizes *Ketty Brövig* (tanker) and *Speybank*. (9) 20.2.41 took tanker *British Advocate* (6,994brt) prize, sent ship to France. (10) 21.2.41 sank neutral Greek freighter *Gregorios* (2,546brt) (false manifest). (11) 21.2.41 sank Canadian merchantman *Canadian Cruiser* (7,178brt). (12) 23.2.41 sank Dutch collier *Rantau Pandjang* (2,542brt). (13) 16.3.41 rendezvous with raider *Kormoran* and *U 124*.

126

25 December 1940 and 2 January 1941 with the raider *Thor*, between 14 and 17 February 1941 with the raider *Atlantis* and on 16 March 1941 with the raider *Kormoran* and *U 124*.

The best-known capture by *Admiral Scheer* was that of the British refrigerator ship *Duquesa* (8,561brt) with a cargo of 14 million eggs and 3,000 tons of frozen meat, intercepted on 18 December 1940 on the Equator and made a prize. Being a coal-burner, her prospects of making a German-held port were poor and she became part of the retinue, sometimes towed by *Nordmark*, and known by all under affectionate titles such as 'The Floating Delicatessen' (British) and 'Wilhelmshaven South Catering Store' (German). Having outlived her usefulness, the ship was sunk on 18 February 1941.

British naval forces spared no effort to bring *Admiral Scheer* to account. In December 1940 three battle groups were involved in the hunt: the cruisers *Dorsetshire* and *Neptune* operating from Freetown; the aircraft carrier *Hermes*, the cruiser *Dragon* and the AMC *Pretoria Castle* around the island of St Helena; and Force K, consisting of the aircraft carrier *Formidable* and the cruiser *Norfolk*. On 22 February 1941 *Admiral Scheer* was located by a shipboard aircraft from HMS *Glasgow*, whereupon the cruisers *Canberra*, *Australia*, *Shropshire*, *Capetown* and *Emerald* and the aircraft carrier *Hermes* were called up, but contact was lost in poor visibility.

On 26–27 March 1941 *Admiral Scheer* broke back through the Denmark Strait, and although sighting the patrolling cruisers *Fiji* and *Nigeria* the ship was not spotted. She was met by the destroyers *Z 23* and *Z 24* and the torpedo-boat *Iltis* off Bergen on the 30th and made fast at Kiel on 1 April 1941, where the C-in-C, Grossadmiral Raeder, came aboard to greet and congratulate the ship's company on their success.

1941

Admiral Scheer entered the Deutsche Werke yard at Kiel for overhaul between 15 April and 1 July and received provisional notice for a second raiding voyage scheduled for July. Following the *Bismarck* disaster and the failed break-out of *Lützow*, however, this was cancelled. Kapitän zur See Wilhelm Meendsen-Bohlken was appointed to be her fifth commander on 12 June. A period of working-up preceded a transfer to Norway from 4 to 8 September, followed by a recall to form part of the so-called 'Baltic Fleet'. Subordinated to Group North, the cruiser sailed from Swinemünde on 23 September in company with the battleship *Tirpitz*, the light cruisers *Nürnberg* and *Köln* and the destroyers *Z 25*, *Z 26* and *Z 27*. During this voyage two

depth charges exploded on deck as the result of crew handling error. *Admiral Scheer* was released from the squadron on 25 September and sailed for the Blohm & Voss yard at Hamburg via the Kiel Canal for urgent engine repairs. She was laid up from 29 September until 24 October and then returned to the Baltic for crew training, interrupted by a further lay-up in the shipyard at Kiel.

1942

On 3 February *Admiral Scheer* negotiated the Kiel Canal to Brunsbüttel. It was planned that she would join up with *Scharnhorst*, *Gneisenau* and *Prinz Eugen* following their 'Channel Dash' from Brest and proceed at once to Norway. However the two battlecruisers were mined during the latter part of their voyage and needed repairs in home waters. Accordingly, only *Prinz Eugen* set off from Brunsbüttel on 20 February with *Admiral Scheer*, escorted by the destroyers *Richard Beitzen*, *Friedrich Ihn*, *Paul Jacobi* and *Z 25* and the torpedo-boat *Seeadler*; the destroyer *Hermann Schoemann* and the torpedo-boat *Iltis* attached themselves to the escort later. The group anchored in Grimstadfjord near Bergen on the 22nd and sailed next day for Narvik. During this latter stage of the voyage, *Prinz Eugen* had her stern blown off by a torpedo from HM Submarine *Trident*, but *Admiral Scheer* reached Lofjord near Trondheim undamaged at midday and idled there for almost three months before making Bogen Bay safely on 10 May in company with *Z 30*, *Z 38*, two torpedo-boats and the oiler *Dithmarschen*. On 25 May she was joined by sister-ship *Lützow*, three more destroyers and the oiler *Nordmark*.

On 4 June these vessels were designated 'No 2 Battle Group' under the command of Vizeadmiral Kummetz, BdK (Befehlshaber der Kreuzer, or C-in-C Cruisers) with his flag aboard *Lützow*. On 2 July the two heavy cruisers and five destroyers moved to Kaafjord to amalgamate with No 1 Battle Group consisting of the battleship *Tirpitz*, flagship of Admiral Schniewind, Fleet C-in-C, the heavy cruiser *Admiral Hipper*, two destroyers and two torpedo-boats. The purpose of assembling this powerful force was Operation 'Rösselsprung' (Knight's Move), aimed at the destruction of Murmansk convoy PQ.17. On 5 July *Tirpitz*, *Admiral Hipper*, *Admiral Scheer* (*Lützow* ran aground before leaving the fjord), seven destroyers and two torpedo-boats headed for the open sea but put back the following day when the participation of the surface forces was cancelled.

Admiral Scheer returned to Bogen Bay with the destroyers *Z 24* and *Friedrich Ihn*, the torpedo-boats *T 15* and *T 17* and the oiler *Dithmarschen* and remained at her moorings in Skommenfjord for several months until the commencement of Operation 'Wunderland' on 16 August. This operation had its origins in a report submitted by Group Command North in July 1942 and which, in referring to the operational situation in Northern Siberian waters, suggested the possibility of action there by the diesel-powered heavy cruisers:

1   Agents have reported that in recent years in the South Kara Sea the port of Anderma has been developed, and the effective destruction of this and the harbour facilities at Murmansk, and disruption to the Kola coastal freighter traffic on-shipping the material brought in convoys from Britain, can be significant. It is assumed that no escort forces will be found east of Archangel, and a rewarding target is offered here for cruisers.

2(a) The special difficulty for naval activities in the Kara and West Siberian Seas is the ice situation, which in recent years has been completely irregular and is dependent on wind and climatic factors.

2(b) Since the B-Dienst is not likely to be able to provide information on the Russian ice situation affecting navigation on the North Siberian sea routes, our own meteorological service in the area is indispensable and the stationing there of special fishing vessels is planned.

3   In operational planning it must be borne in mind that the area is much broader than the North Sea and the distance to be covered for an attack around Novaya Zemlya to the Siberian mainland coast requires several days for the voyage out and back. A withdrawal into some remote part of the waters using the great radius of action of the cruiser must be disregarded in the circumstances. Enemy response in our operational area is improbable, but the possibility of ambush during the return must be reckoned with. Unobserved sailing and a surprise appearance in the operational area is important. There is no possibility of destroyer escort on refuelling grounds and because they would be a burden in unfavourable ice conditions in the operational area.

This feasibility study was well received at SKL and resulted in the plan for Operation 'Wunderland' being drawn up. In addition to the usual instructions contained in the orders issued to the commanders of the two former Panzerschiffe were the following riders:

(a)   The code-name 'Wunderland' for this operation characterises the fact that it takes us into completely unknown territory.

(b)   Task: attack on shipping in the Kara Sea. Principal target convoys with preference for those arriving from the east. Liberty for coastal bombardments.

(c)   In addition to *Admiral Scheer* two U-boats will be involved in place of the fishing vessels.

(d)   The element of surprise is essential for the success of the operation. Therefore maintain the greatest possible wireless silence and remain out of sight. On account of incomplete information strict guidelines not given. Exception: only justifiable risks are to be taken.

(e)   Deployment of the U-boats: one boat ice reconnaissance in the northern passage north of Novaya Zemlya to the ice limit, second boat scout towards Bjelyg and Port Dickson, islands of the West Siberian Sea.

Towards midday on 16 August *Admiral Scheer* left her fjord with *Friedrich Eckholdt, Erich Steinbrinck* and *Richard Beitzen* as escorts and passed the North Cape on a heading for Bear Island and Franz Josef Land. Towards Bear Island the destroyers were released and the cruiser continued alone. The two U-boats detailed for the mission were *U 601* (Kapitänleutnant Peter Grau) and *U 251* (Korvettenkapitän Heinrich Timm). The shipboard aircraft was kept aloft for reconnaissance. The further east *Admiral Scheer* progressed the thicker she found the ice-field, and numerous icebergs were encountered. Variable winds, depending on their direction, brought fog, mist or clear visibility. The drift ice was so thick in places that the cruiser had to manoeuvre with great caution to avoid becoming iced-in, and to protect the propellers against damage. With her powerful engines she succeeded in escaping whenever endangered, and on the single occasion when the ship became trapped she forced a way clear. Towards noon on the eighth day of the voyage a lone ship, the ice-breaker *Alexander Sibirijakow*, was sighted and when ordered to stop with a shot across her bows returned fire and had to be sunk. As this vessel had wirelessed, *Admiral Scheer's* mission was compromised and the commander was compelled to elect immediately either:

1   To undertake commerce warfare on the sea routes between Port Dickson to the Strait of Novaya Zemlya in the area of the Jugor Strait, or

2   To execute new operations in the sense of the

operational orders by carrying out attacks on important coastal points.

Kapitän zur See Meedsen-Bohlken chose option 2, an attack on Port Dickson. Lacking adequate charts and navigational information about the waters, recourse was had to an old English Mercator Projection chart to 1:200,000 scale. The harbour and shore installations were subjected to concentric fire, to which the coastal batteries made an ineffective reply. After disengaging, *Admiral Scheer* headed north to wireless home her report and met up with *U 255* (Kapitänleutnant Reinhard Reche) north of Novaya Zemlya for meteorological and ice reports. The commander was then ordered to return by Admiral Polar Seas and met the same three-destroyer escort off Bear Island, anchoring at Bogen Bay on 30 August.

Group North recorded: 'The operation penetrated into completely new territory about which only incomplete information existed, presenting the commander with a task which involved unknown difficulties ahead. The operation was carried out with enthusiasm, skill, reflection and obvious determination and deserves full recognition.'

SKL observed: 'Under especially adverse conditions, an operation carried out boldly, prudently and with great success. On several occasions the ship was in a very difficult ice situation. The operation against Port Dickson with regard to navigational difficulties (inadequate charts) [was] especially recognised.'

Admiral Scheer remained in Norway during September and October, alternating on occasions between anchorages. In November she received instructions to return to Germany and on the 6th sailed from Trondheim with *Z 23*, *Z 28* and *Z 29*, all four units arriving safely at Swinemünde on the 10th. In late December the cruiser docked at Wilhelmshaven for a long overdue engine and armaments overhaul. Fregattenkapitän Ernst Gruber acted as caretaker commander from November until January 1943.

1943

During the course of the dockyard lay-up a new commander, Kapitän zur See Richard Rothe-Roth was appointed on 1 February and 50 per cent of the crew were replaced. *Admiral Scheer* was not even at AA readiness, and the auxiliary machinery had been returned to the manufacturers for renovation. Because of the comprehensive crew changes the ship would have to work up from scratch, and instruction was limited to 'dry training'.

By this time streams of Allied bombers were arriving over the Reich day and night while the Luftwaffe, thinly spread across thousands of miles of front line, was less and less able to make a decisive intervention. On 26 February, during the second of two air raids on Wilhelmshaven that day, a mixed RAF/USAAF force of 60–70 four-engine aircraft dropped 207 HE bombs of various sizes from an altitude of 6,000–7,000m on the docks and harbour installations. Advance warning had been given at 1052, but an unfavourable wind was responsible for the attempted smoke screens failing to deploy correctly. *Admiral Scheer*, in drydock V, was therefore a clear target. She was hit by one bomb which failed to explode, and ten others went off in Docks IV and VI, from which the cruiser received splinter damage. Important areas of the shipyard itself escaped lightly, a few lighters and smaller auxiliary craft being sunk. The death toll aboard *Admiral Scheer* was one crewman. The raid as a whole cost the lives of four Navy men plus an Italian in the Flak control centre, and fourteen civilians. Fifty people were wounded, eight of them Wehrmacht personnel.

For a raid to be concentrated wholly on the dockyard suggested that *Admiral Scheer* had been the target and that similar raids would follow. Accordingly the commander received orders to make the ship seaworthy as soon as possible for transfer to Swinemünde. This was achieved within fourteen days. A full Flak complement was aboard when she sailed in a half-finished condition replete with all the deficiencies of a dockyard lay-up. She reached her destination safely, the highest praise being accorded her crew, half of whom had had the benefit of no more than the briefest shipboard training.

The remaining repairs were difficult to carry out at Swinemünde, which had no drydock and few installations such as cranes and workshops, but miracles were achieved as a result of collaboration between shipyard and crew, and it was soon possible to commence crew training.

Following the fiasco in the Barents Sea at the end of 1942 which had resulted in Hitler's decommissioning order for the heavy units, *Admiral Scheer,* after partially working up, was attached to the newly formed Fleet Training Group whose main task it was to train cadets. This was achieved by embarking up to 500 cadets at a time to do the work of members of the permanent company they displaced. Within a few months these officer recruits were supposed to learn everything necessary to stand them in good stead during their future careers. This work continued into 1944.

1944

During the summer *Admiral Scheer* visited Copenhagen for a few days but spent the remainder of time at sea with short calls along the Baltic coast, particularly at Goten-hafen. On 9 October she had just left that port when Eighth Air Force heavy bombers attacked vessels at their moorings and sank the hospital ship *Stuttgart*.

The year continued with cadet training and its attendant rapid turnover, every effort being made to keep the ship at full war readiness. On land the German Army was in retreat against an enemy many times superior in numbers, and the Kriegsmarine was requested to support the defence by shore bombardment. After two extra 3.7cm twin Flak guns had been fitted at short notice at Gotenhafen, *Admiral Scheer* sailed for Sworbe in company with the destroyers *Z 25* and *Z 35* and the torpedo-boats *T 3*, *T 5*, *T 9*, *T 12*, *T 13* and *T 16*. Between 22 and 24 November the group concentrated fire on Soviet positions and armoured columns, thus enabling the German defences to evacuate the peninsula without suffering heavy losses. During the operation in the narrow channels off Sworbe the ship came under repeated attack by Soviet bombers and torpedo aircraft. Two torpedoes missed narrowly and all bombs were near-misses except for a single hit on the upper deck above Compartment XVI which failed to explode or penetrate the decking. The shipboard Ar 196 was shot down by Russian fighters.

At the termination of the Sworbe operation the cruiser returned to Gotenhafen because of a fuel shortage but remained at full readiness.

1945

Once the major Soviet offensive developed from the Baranow bridgehead in mid-January, greatly superior enemy numbers now threatened Reich territory itself, and the few available units of the Kriegsmarine became involved repeatedly as floating artillery batteries in actions against Russian assembly points and advancing columns. After having spent most of January at Pillau, *Admiral Scheer* engaged in these duties from 2 to 5 February off the Samland coast in company with the torpedo-boats *T 23*, *T 35* and *T 36* and from the 9th to the 10th of the month off Frauenburg with *Z 34*, *T 23*, *T 28* and *T 36*.

At 2300 on 18 February at Pillau *Admiral Scheer* made fast astern of the night fighter direction ship *Togo* while her stern was towed round to bring her full broadside to bear shoreward. Before dawn on the 19th she opened fire with all 28cm guns and the port 15cm battery in support of the German land offensive to re-open the Königsberg–Pillau land corridor for the escape of refugees. Retiring offshore at first light, the cruiser returned at the same time the following morning and bombarded Soviet positions

for two hours from 0500, the objective thereby being achieved.

The cruiser's other tasks included the care of refugees, protecting the over-full hospital trains and ships and rendering assistance to wounded and refugees boarding these latter and other craft. Almost anything that would float was pressed into service. A small shore party went to the Schichau yard at Elbing to arrange for the incomplete torpedo-boat hulls there to be towed westwards.

Off Elbing itself on 6 February, *Admiral Scheer* bombarded the Russian lines at a range of 35km. The ammunition expended amounted to 915 rounds of 28cm and 87 rounds of 15cm. In a similar operation at Pillau in a two-hour period, 160 rounds of 28cm and 121 rounds of 15cm were fired, and in a later bombardment 90 rounds of 28cm and 25 rounds of 15cm.

As the result of this continued gunnery all barrels were in urgent need of a re-bore (in fact, since commissioning the usage had always exceeded the prescribed barrel life). As the only workshop and machinery for the task were at Kiel, the cruiser sailed for the port on 8 March, calling in at Gotenhafen to take on board 800 refugees and 200 wounded. On 9 March, off Bornholm, the commander was warned that it was unsafe to proceed as he would have to negotiate an uncleared minefield, and he took the ship to Swinemünde to disembark his passengers, where *Admiral Scheer* was at once pressed into service to assist the Army and in the course of the next few days bombarded Soviet positions between Kolberg and Dievenow, the ammunition expended being 200 rounds of 28cm and 547 rounds of 15cm. As there was no 28cm ammunition at Swinemünde, the cruiser sailed for Kiel on 16 March with a fresh intake of 400 refugees and wounded. On 18 March she made fast in the fitting-out basin of the Deutsche Werke near the cruisers *Admiral Hipper* and *Emden*.

At this time Allied bomber fleets over Germany were operating virtually unopposed in the air and threatened from the ground only by widely scattered anti-aircraft concentrations. The civilian populations of the cities sheltered in cellars, air raid bunkers and the ruins. On docking, *Admiral Scheer* unshipped her Flak guns and ammunition. The heavy armament was unserviceable because of the proposed barrel changeovers. 'B' turret completed the exchange on 8 April, and because of the constant air attacks the commander was proposing to move out into Heikendorf Bay on the 10th and have a floating crane assist in the exchange of 'A' turret's barrels. Some of the ship's company had been given furlough and most of the cadets had been disembarked, and the complement of shipboard personnel was very much reduced in consequence.

At 2150 on 9 April there was an air-raid warning and most of the remaining crewmen went to bunkers ashore, leaving aboard only the 90 or so officers and men of the damage control parties, which included command relay, fire-fighting and electrical plant personnel. The first bombs began falling at 2230 and the ship was first hit at 2238. At 2245 hits caused the lighting and command relay systems to fail and the cruiser assumed a list of 16 degrees to starboard, but power was restored long enough to get the ground vents open and make compensatory flooding to halt the list at 18 degrees. At just after 2245, as a consequence of further hits and near-misses, the list increased quickly to 28 degrees, at which point the engineer officer of the watch, Oberleutnant Strempel, gave the command to leave the electrical plant running and abandon ship. This order did not reach all centres because of electrical failure, although individual posts were abandoned as soon as the gravity of the situation became apparent.

Climbing through burning and smoke-filled rooms to reach companionways and portholes, some cewmen were killed or injured by falling machinery and components. Despite the asphyxiating conditions and their exhaustion, groups dragged injured and unconscious shipmates to safety, those not being able to swim the few strokes to the quayside being picked up in the water by small craft. Salvage workers from *Emden* cut into the hull in several places and rescue teams scoured the upturned hull for 42 hours in the search of further survivors.

Having discharged her ammunition and fuel, *Admiral Scheer* was high out of the water and ballasted with only 600m³ of seawater in the double bottom. She capsized over a period of about 12 to 17 minutes in 15m of water, the primary cause being a large gash on the starboard side caused by near-misses. All eight members of Damage Control Party I and seven other crew members, including three engineer cadets, were left entombed in the mangled remains of the ship.

Work on breaking up the wreck began in July 1945 under the supervision of the British authorities. All valuable metals and the gunhouses and turrets were removed before the bare torso of the ship was abandoned where she lay. When work commenced on the new naval arsenal, the remains were covered over with rubble to become the foundations for a large car park.

Right: Panzerschiff 'B' under construction on the stocks at Wilhelmshaven.

Top: Panzerschiff 'B' a few days before launching. In the foreground are Drydocks II and III.

Above: The VIPs arrive on launch day, 1 April 1933. From the left, Admiral Förster, C-in-C Fleet; in the act of saluting, Reich War Minister Generaloberst von Blomberg and Admiral Raeder, C-in-C Naval Command; and right, with open greatcoat lapels, Konteradmiral Massmann, Senior Shipyard Manager.

Right: The act of christening, performed by Frau Marianne Besserer, daughter of the late Admiral Scheer, shattering the obligatory bottle of champagne against the stem of the hull. The vertical numbers run to the keel and indicate the ship's draught in feet, doubled.

Opposite page: *Admiral Scheer* slowly gathers momentum as she slides into her element. The rain has not deterred the thousands of spectators who always attended these launchings.

Opposite page: Dressed overall, *Admiral Scheer* slides down the greased slipways and her stern immerses until sufficient buoyancy is available to float the hull – the critical moment of all launchings.

Left: The massive prefabricated, pagoda-like bridge structure before its installation. At the top is the foretop platform; below is the searchlight platform. In the background, right, the stern of the third Panzerschiff can just be seen on the slip.

Below: *Admiral Scheer* seen completing across the end of Slipways 1 and 2; scaffolding for Panzerschiff 'C', under construction, can be seen off the bow. In the left foreground is South Quay, where there is a small floating dock and, nearby, a lightship.

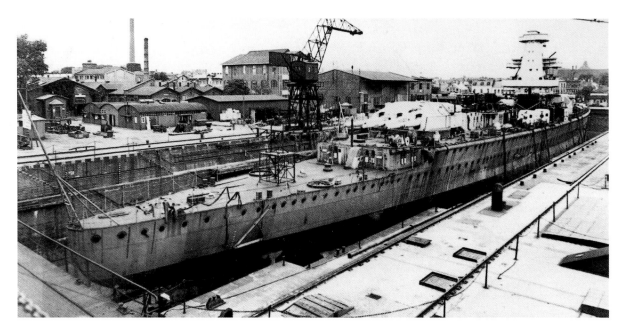

Above: *Admiral Scheer* fitting out in Drydock IV. The bridge structure and both main triple turrets have been shipped and are complete. Several 15cm gunhouses have been installed on the starboard side. Note the huge ensign staff at the stern.
Below: Fitting out along the quay. In this photograph the 'Langer Heinrich' floating crane lowers another of the 28cm guns into its cradle in 'A' turret.

Above: *Admiral Scheer* in Jade Bay, Wilhelmshaven, during one of her early engine trials. No weapons control equipment has yet been fitted.

Below left: When *Admiral Scheer* was accepted in the Reichsmarine on 12 November 1934 the 1906-vintage *Braunschweig* class pre-dreadnought *Hessen* was decommissioned at the same time and her crew transferred aboard the new ship. This view shows *Hessen*'s company paraded on the quarterdeck for the decommissioning cere-mony, with *Admiral Scheer* astern. In the foreground are the two 28cm guns of the old battleship's rear turret.

Below right: The decommissioned *Hessen* seen from the roof of 'B' turret. *Admiral Scheer* is in commission, as evidenced by the Reichsmarine flag flying at the ensign staff.

Above left: *Admiral Scheer*'s forepeak, showing one of the two bow anchors and the ship's armorial shield with the inscription 'Skagerrak' (Jutland). Later the diagonal was changed to run from bottom left to upper right.
Above right: A view of midships, port side, in August 1935. A shipboard crane is seen lowering a pinnace alongside.

Below: *Admiral Scheer*, still lacking all weapons direction systems, on trials in the Baltic in the summer of 1934.
Right: At moorings, Kiel, January 1935. A floating crane is alongside, probably for the installation of heavy gear. The foretop 10.5cm rangefinder has not yet been fitted.

Left: Looking astern over the anchor cluse near the forepeak towards 'A' turret and the battle-mast with its searchlights and bridge platforms. The chain of the second bow anchor is seen at the right.

Above: Two sailing dinghies review the completed *Admiral Scheer* at Kiel. Both main rangefinders (foretop and aft command centre) have now been installed.

Below: *Admiral Scheer* from the air in the summer of 1935.

Above: The public queues to visit the ship on an Open Day in June 1935. The ship is made fast port side to quay. This photograph provides a good view of an 8.8cm twin, two 15cm gunhouses and platforms at the rear of the bridge structure.

Below: *Admiral Scheer* at Wilhelmshaven, 15 September 1935. The presence of so many civilians on the quayside suggests that a long voyage is in the offing. On the opposite bank of the river is the fitting-out quay, with the old battleship *Schleswig-Holstein* alongside.

Right, upper: *Admiral Scheer* at Kiel. 'B' turret seems enormous from this stern angle. Note also the torpedo tubes on the quarterdeck, the deployed propeller guards and the extended mooring boom forward.

Right, lower: *Admiral Scheer* at sea in her original configuration but with the armorial shield altered. At the ensign staff is the new Reich flag, introduced aboard all naval units on 7 November 1935.

Above: Starboard amidships, with good detail: a cutter swung out, the shipboard He 60 floatplane on the catapult, the searchlight platform around the funnel mantle and aerial outriggers above and the individual platforms on the battle mast. The 15cm gunhouses are traversed forward abeam, indicating that the crews are being exercised.

Right: Free time was often spent sunbathing on the upper deck. This photograph provides an excellent view of the massive battle-mast structure and 'A' turret, which bore the name 'Lützow'.

Right: The ship's laundrymen ironing. Ships of this size had everything necessary aboard for the upkeep of the uniform issue – laundries, ironing rooms, tailors, shoemakers, etc.

Right: A crewman's locker in the accommodation deck. Despits its small size, much could be stowed within if the regulations (which were very precise) were followed. Other storage places and lockers were available for bulkier items of gear. The small boxes, known as 'utensil cases', seen on the top of the locker were supplied for shoe brushes and polish plus materials for patching and darning which accompanied a man throughout his service.

Right: The He 60 floatplane on the ship's crane. These aircraft had a Luftwaffe pilot and a Kriegsmarine observer. Here the pilot is standing on the fuselage and the observer on one of the floats.

Left, upper: *Admiral Scheer* dressed overall and flying the Reich battle ensign at the foretop, seen at a mooring buoy at Kiel after her first refit, probably during People's Navy Week in June 1936. An admiral's bridge has been added to the battle-mast.

Left, lower: *Admiral Scheer* at the Naval Review in the presence of Hitler in Kiel Bay, 29 May 1936. This was the week in which the Laboe naval memorial was dedicated, coinciding with the twentieth anniversary of the Battle of Jutland.

Above: *Admiral Scheer*'s crew line the starboard rail from stem to stern at the Naval Review of 29 May 1936.

Right: Approaching a lock gate on the Kiel Canal: a view of the bows from the bridge. On the foredeck and port side several cable parties have been fallen in preparatory to making fast.

Above: A meeting at sea with sister-ship *Deutschland*, from which this photograph was taken.

Right: Barrels of lubricating oil are brought aboard by crane during a winter replenishment exercise off the Spanish coast.

Above: *Admiral Scheer* at Swinemünde between Spanish operations in 1937 or 1938, displaying striped markings in the national colours across the armoured roofs of the main turrets.
Right: *Admiral Scheer* off Spain in a near-gale.

Above: A broadside view of *Admiral Scheer* at anchor in mid-1939. Rigged from the battle-mast yardarm is the 'anchor ball' and from the funnel outrigger a triangular device indicating that the ship is not under way. The starboard mooring boom has been extended and the aft accommodation ladder let down, the Reich flag is hoisted at the ensign staff and a swastika flag flutters at the forepeak.

Below: The two triangular symbols set on the funnel outrigger shrouds indicate that the rudder is amidships. Yellow diamonds were hoisted at various heights to advise engine telegraph orders.

Right: Signalling gear used during formation steaming. *Fahrtbälle* are yellow diamond shapes hoisted on outrigger wires and used to indicate engine speed: low on the wire indicates slow ahead, midway indicates half-ahead and top indicates full ahead. When an engine is stopped, the yellow diamond shapes are replaced by the rectangular *Stoppball*. *Ruderbälle* are rudder symbols. One inverted triangle is coloured red (port), the other, with apex upwards, is green (starboard). When both triangle devices are hoisted level half way up the wire, the rudder is fore-and-aft. When the red triangle is high and the green triangle low, the rudder is hard to port; when vice versa it is hard to starboard.

Kommandantenwimpel = commander's streamer; *Konteradmiral-/Admiralsflagge* = Rear-Admiral's/Admiral's command flag; *Kommodorestander* = Commodore's pennant.

Below: *Admiral Scheer* (nearest camera) and *Gneisenau* seen from *Deutschland* during the 1939 fleet gunnery exercises. Notice the lowered railing stanchions and ensign staff on the quarterdeck, the two smoke buoys and, in the right foreground, the mounting for a 2cm Flak gun, the weapon having been unshipped for protection from the elements.

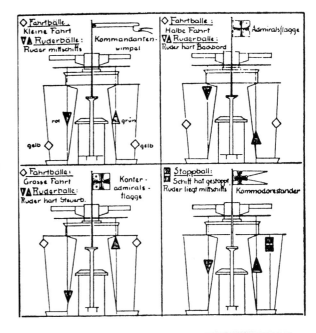

151

Left, upper: Shortly after the outbreak of war the RAF made a number of bombing raids on German ports. On 4 September 1939 they tried their luck in the German Bight. This imaginative 'eye-witness' sketch appeared in the *Illustrated London News*. Although *Admiral Scheer* was hit by three 500lb bombs, in fact they all failed to explode. Flak accounted for one of the bombers.

Left, lower: *Admiral Scheer* was absent from the Norwegian campaign of April 1940, undergoing an extensive refit at Wilhelmshaven. In this photograph the ship, now reclassified as a heavy cruiser, is seen in Drydock IV. The bridge structure is in the process of being dismantled to make way for a tower mast similar to that fitted aboard *Deutschland*.

Above: Installation of the new tubular mast aboard *Admiral Scheer* by the floating crane 'Langer Heinrich'. The foretop, which would later accommodate the main gunnery control centre, is prominent.

Left, upper: It seems scarcely possible that this relatively thin tube could be strong enough to support all platforms, fittings and appurtenances of the battle-mast without difficulty. In the background *Tirpitz* is fitting out alongside South Quay.

Left, lower: *Admiral Scheer* at East Quay with the floating crane manoeuvring the new battle-mast for lowering aboard.

Above: The heavy cruiser nearing completion of her major refit.

Right: *Admiral Scheer*'s stern and 'B' turret ('Friedrich der Grosse') seen during a cold spell in the spring of 1940, during the ship's conversion.

Above: The reconstructed *Admiral Scheer* makes her début on an inshore voyage (as indicated by the Reich war flag at the ensign staff) in Jade Bay. The most striking changes are the new battle-mast, the modified bows, the radar installation at the foretop, the new mainmast abaft the funnel and the slightly raked funnel cap.

Right: The new foretop, showing the 10.5cm rangefinder, single searchlight and forward Flak control centre.

Above and right: After a highly successful commerce raiding cruise of five months' duration which extended to the Antarctic and Indian Oceans, on 1 April 1941 *Admiral Scheer* returned unscathed to Kiel, where the crew were greeted by the C-in-C of the Kriegsmarine, Grossadmiral Raeder. The upper photograph shows the cruiser on her arrival; that on the right shows her complement of cadets mustered for inspection.

Above: The usual inspection lay-up followed at Deutsche Werke and the cruiser was later recalled from Norway to form part of the 'Baltic Fleet'. In this photograph, probably taken from *Tirpitz*, *Admiral Scheer* is in line ahead of the light cruisers *Leipzig* and *Nürnberg* and destroyers.

Below: A warrant officer and ratings pose near 'A' turret. Note the 2cm quadruple AA on the turret roof, the twin 10.5cm serving as a heavy Flak amidships, the open visor of the 10.5cm 'A' turret rangefinder and, behind it, on the bridge face, a square Marx survival float.

Above and below: Following the successful Channel Dash by *Scharnhorst*, *Gneisenau* and *Prinz Eugen* from Brest to Germany in February 1942, *Admiral Scheer* and *Prinz Eugen* were detailed to transfer at once to Norway. These two photographs were taken aboard *Prinz Eugen* during the voyage: *Admiral Scheer* off her starboard quarter (above) and following astern (below). Notice the pronounced rake to *Admiral Scheer*'s funnel cap and the quadruple Flak mounting on *Prinz Eugen*'s quarterdeck.

Above left: *Admiral Scheer* running in Norwegian inshore waters.

Above: Operation 'Wunderland', late August 1942. Seen in the crosswires of the targeting optic is the Soviet ice-breaker *Alexander Sibirijakow*, ablaze and sinking in the Kara Sea after an exchange of fire with the German cruiser.

Left: *Admiral Scheer*'s battle-mast, with a FuMO 27 and FuMB 7 Timor radar aerial aloft and a FuMB 4 Sumatra on the arms of the rangefinder. On the bridge bulkhead is a raft with paddle, and on the platform below a 3.7cm twin Flak.

Right, upper: *Admiral Scheer* under camouflage netting in a Norwegian fjord, firing her 10.5cm Flak to ward off a developing air attack.

Right, lower: The anchorages of the German units were frequently changed to keep the enemy 'on the hop'. A small supply ship has come alongside the cruiser, which appears to have tree-scape camouflage on the foredeck.

Left: *Admiral Scheer* in Norway. The ship's company is mustered by division on the foredeck. Note the radar aerials facing abeam (as was normal when not in use), the two rafts on the bridge face and the dazzle camouflage of the superstructure.

Right: *Admiral Scheer* broadside in mid-fjord at Skjomen near Narvik, photographed from one of the numerous auxiliary warships present.

Below: An Allied aerial reconnaissance photograph of the German cruiser inside her anti-torpedo netting at Bogen Bay near Narvik.

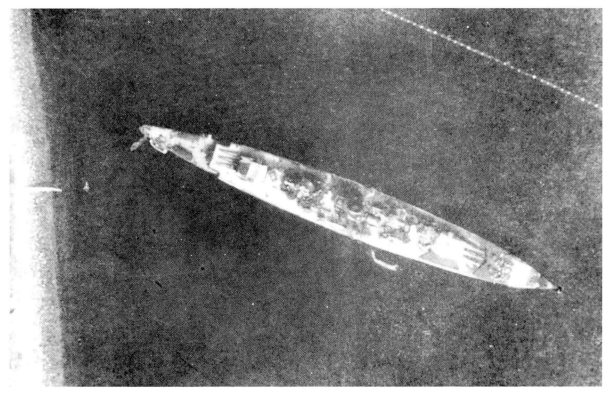

Left: A fine aerial photograph of *Admiral Scheer* within her net defences, taken by the shipboard Arado 196.
Above: A photograph showing the pronounced rake to the funnel cap, the Ar 196 floatplane on its catapult and the two large radar mattresses at the foretop.

Below: *Admiral Scheer* in home waters, late 1944. Another radar aerial has been installed – above the rangefinder of the after command centre.

Left: Two further photographs of *Admiral Scheer* in 1944–45, showing the large (2 × 6m) radar aerials at the foretop and after command centre.

Above: *Admiral Scheer* in 1945 in the Gotenhafen roadstead.

Right, upper: The cruiser enters the sea canal at Pillau prior to one of the two shore bombardments of Soviet armoured formations. In the background, right, is the night-fighter direction ship *Togo*.

Right, lower: The ship made a fateful return to Kiel for a rebore for her main armament. On 9 April 1945, during a massive air attack on the city, *Admiral Scheer* was hit and capsized. This Allied reconnaissance photograph shows the cruiser lying keel-up alongside in the harbour basin.

Above left: The capsized hull photographed shortly after the end of the war.

Left: An aerial view of the devastated dock area; most shipyard buildings are in ruins, although the floating crane survives upright near the stern of the inverted heavy cruiser. The tongue of land running behind the foreshore was part of the naval arsenal. In the background the estuary is strewn with wrecks, amongst which (left) is the capsized hull of the former passenger liner *New York*. To the right is the 'Kilian' U-boat bunker of the Howaldtswerke.

Above: The Deutsche Werke, Kiel. At the top edge of the illustration is the capsized *Admiral Scheer*, in the centre the shipbuilding basin. In the left foreground is the 'Konrad' U-boat bunker; in the first of two adjacent drydocks is the wreck of the minelayer *Brummer* (ex Norwegian *Olav Tryggvason*) and in the next a Type XXI U-boat and the Type IX/C40 boat *U 1227*, seriously damaged on 9 April 1945 and scuttled by explosive charges on 3 May 1945.

Above and below: The renaissance of Kiel Dockyard in the early 1950s with the beginning of the first rebuilding work. The remains of the cannibalised *Admiral Scheer* were covered with rubble to become the foundations for a large car park.

Panzerschiff *Admiral Graf Spee*

Origin of the Name

Maximilian Johannes Maria Hubertus, Reichsgraf von Spee (born in Copenhagen on 22 June 1861) was the son of Rhenish landed gentry. He entered the Imperial Navy as a cadet on 23 April 1878 and was commissioned on 17 December 1881. He attained Flag Officer rank as Konteradmiral von Spee on 27 January 1910 and at the time of his last promotion, to Vizeadmiral on 15 November 1913, he was made C-in-C of the German East Asia Cruiser Squadron and will always be remembered in connection with its tragic destiny.

The Squadron was based at Tsingtau, a German enclave on the Chinese mainland. It was considered untenable in war, and in August 1914 a group consisting of the

Below: Vizeadmiral Maximilian Graf von Spee.

13,000-ton (eight 21cm gun) heavy cruisers *Scharnhorst* (flagship) and *Gneisenau* and the light cruiser *Nürnberg* removed to Ponape in the Caroline Islands before setting out for the coast of Chile. The light cruisers *Dresden* and *Leipzig* joined the group at Easter Island. The Squadron was served by a sizeable number of colliers, and Germany's enemies – Britain, France and Japan – had several task forces at sea hunting down the latter.

On 1 November 1914, near the Santa Maria Islands off Coronel, Chile, the German Squadron came across one of the British cruiser divisions. In the ensuing battle the armoured cruisers HMS *Good Hope* (flagship of Admiral Craddock) and HMS *Monmouth* were sunk without loss to the German force. A British light cruiser, pre-dreadnought battleship and AMC escaped.

The triumphant German units put into Valparaiso, Chile, where, it is rumoured, they were offered internment by the German authorities: because of the naval victory, it would not have been held dishonourable, but if that was the case von Spee declined it.

The Imperial Navy had arranged for 67,000 tons of coal to be made available for an unknown purpose – from 5 December 1914 20,000 tons each at La Plata, Argentina and New York, and a further 15,000 tons at New York and 12,000 tons at the Canary Islands as from 20 January 1915. This suggests that the von Spee had the intention of attempting a break-through to Germany even though he had a serious shortfall of ammunition which could not be made good.* The Squadron had fired off half its stock at Coronel and the deficiency was dangerous; nevertheless, von Spee rounded Cape Horn and headed north. Between 0930 and

---

* This suggestion is at variance with Winston Churchill's statement in his book *World in Crisis*. Churchill declared that the German squadron was closing in to occupy the Falklands with heavily armed storm troops on their decks. What else can explain why the squadron was passing inshore of these enemy islands when supposedly heading for Germany? Probably von Spee was not offered internment at Valparaiso, but given instead this audacious mission to capture the Falklands as a fortified German naval base, for reasons which the author himself makes in the concluding paragraph of this volume. —Trans.

1000 in the morning of 8 December 1914 *Gneisenau* and *Nürnberg* approached to within a few miles of the southeast tip of the Falkland Islands and were sighted at Fort Williams, where the modern battlecruisers HMS *Invincible* and HMS *Inflexible* and the cruisers *Kent*, *Carnarvon* and *Cornwall* lay at anchor. The British force put to sea, and, after a long running fight against hopeless odds, *Scharnhorst*, *Gneisenau*, *Leipzig* and *Nürnberg* were all sunk with heavy loss of life that evening. Vizeadmiral von Spee went down aboard his flagship, from which there were no survivors, and his sons Leutnant zur See Otto Ferdinand von Spee and Leutnant zur See Heinrich Franz von Spee also found a sailor's grave, aboard *Nürnberg* and *Gneisenau* respectively.

Admiral Graf Spee: Prewar Career

The Reichswehr Ministry gave approval for the construction of the third ship of the *Deutschland* class on 23 August 1932 and the keel of Panzerschiff 'C' ('Replacement *Braunschweig*') was laid on Slip 2 at the Navy Yard, Wilhelmshaven, on 1 October, the prepared material being transferred to Slip 1 immediately after the launch of *Admiral Scheer* on 1 April 1933. The hull was launched on 30 June 1934. Admiral Raeder delivered the pre-launch speech, and the baptism was performed by Gräfin Huberta von Spee, daughter of the late Admiral. On 6 January 1936 the ship was commissioned by Kapitän zur See Conrad Patzig.

After completion of the usual preliminary trials and intensive working-up, the ship joined the Fleet on 9 April 1936 and functioned as the Fleet flagship at the Kiel Naval Review of 29 May that year, when Hitler dedicated the new naval memorial at Laboe.

Compass adjustment and gunnery trials were carried out between 6 and 26 June off the Canaries. The ship made three patrols to Spanish waters under the international agreement – between 20 August and 9 October 1936 (Wilhelmshaven–Kiel), from 13 December 1936 to 14 February 1937 (Wilhelmshaven–Kiel) and from 2 March to 6 May 1937 (Kiel–Kiel) – following which she represented the Reich at the Spithead Naval Review between 15 and 22 May 1937 on the occasion of the coronation of King George VI. A fourth Spanish patrol was made from 23 June to 7 August 1937 (Kiel–Kiel). *Admiral Graf Spee* took part in the 1937 autumn naval exercises as Fleet flagship, calling at Wisby, Sweden, for three days from 18 September and Kristiansand, Norway, for two days from 1 December under Kapitän zur See Walter Warzecha, who had assumed command on 2 October.

The fifth and last Spanish patrol lasted from 7 to 18 February 1938 (Kiel–Kiel). The Norwegian fjords were visited between 29 June and 9 July 1938, and *Admiral Graf Spee* was at Kiel on 22 August that year for the launching of the heavy cruiser *Prinz Eugen* in the presence of Hitler and Admiral Horthy, the Hungarian Regent. She took part in the autumn naval exercises as Fleet flagship. A refit followed, in which six 8.8cm twin Flak guns were exchanged for six 10.5cm Flak guns on the same chassis, a mattress for an FMG G(gO) (FuMO 22 type) radar was installed on the rangefinder of the foretop revolving dome, the octagonal foretop was reshaped and the single-searchlight platforms either side of the tower mast were replaced by a single-searchlight platform on the forward face of the tower.

Atlantic cruises were made from 6 to 23 October and from 10 to 24 November 1938, with calls at Tangier, Vigo and Portugalete, the last under the ship's third and last commander, Kapitän zur See Hans Langsdorff, who was appointed on 1 November 1938.

Admiral Graf Spee was based at Wilhelmshaven from 1 January 1939. Between 22 and 24 March the Panzerschiff was flagship of the naval force at Memel when the territory was reincorporated into the German Reich (although Hitler voyaged aboard *Deutschland*).

In April 1939 the Fleet C-in-C, Admiral Boehm, raised his flag aboard *Admiral Graf Spee* for the large-scale Atlantic naval exercises in which *Gneisenau* and all three 'pocket battleships' took part, together with numerous other units. From 29 to 31 May the ship was at Hamburg to welcome the Legion Kondor arriving home from Spain aboard KdF ('Strength through Joy') passenger liners.

Admiral Graf Spee at War

Equipped for commerce warfare, on 21 August 1939 *Admiral Graf Spee* left Wilhelmshaven for a remote waiting position south of the Equator and spent a nervous period of inactivity there until 26 September, when Langsdorff received instructions to proceed against enemy merchant shipping. The naval oiler *Altmark* had left Wilhelmshaven on 9 August, and after filling her storage tanks to the brim with diesel oil at Port Arthur, Texas, on 22 August joined Langsdorff off Brazil. Subsequently *Altmark* refuelled the warship on nine occasions, including 28 August, 13 and 20 September, once in November and 6 December – the last time the two ships were together. On several of these occasions Merchant Navy prisoners were taken aboard the tanker. Within a period of less than two months *Admi-*

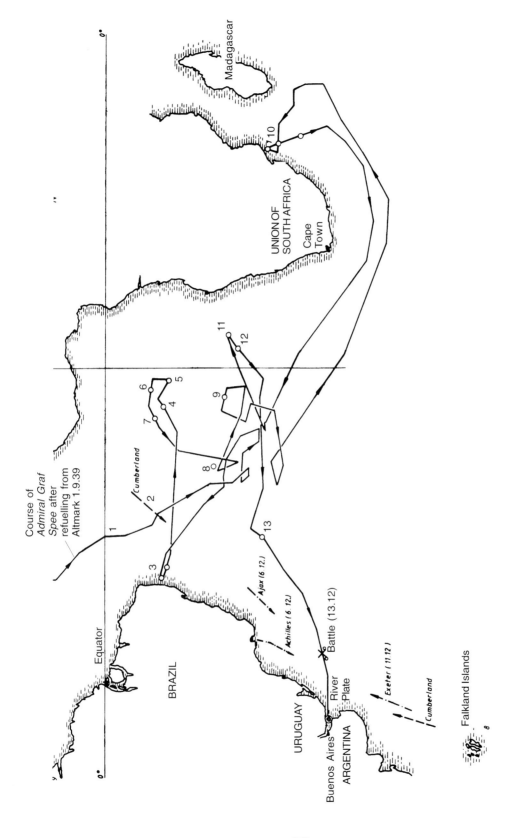

Admiral Graf Spee's commerce-raiding voyage, September–December 1939
Key: (1) 1.9.39 Refuelling rendezvous with *Altmark*. (2) While refuelling from *Altmark* 11.9.39 ship's aircraft spots HMS *Cumberland*. Two German ships proceed together during waiting period in company until 27.9.39. (3) 30.9.39 sinks *Clement*. (4) 5.10.39 *Newton Beech* taken as prize and proceeds with *Graf Spee*. (5) 7.10.39 sinks *Ashlea*. (6) 8.10.39 sinks prize *Newton Beech*. (7) 9.10.39 *Huntsman* taken as prize and proceeds with *Graf Spee*, which meets *Altmark* 14.10.39. (8) 18.10.39 sinks prize *Huntsman* and parts company with *Altmark*. (9) 22.10.39 sinks *Trevanion*. (10) 15.11.39 sinks *Africa Shell*. (11) 2.12.39 sinks *Doric Star*. (12) 5.12.39 sinks *Tairoa*. (13) 7.12.39 sinks *Streonshalh*.

173

ral Graf Spee sank nine merchant vessels totalling 50,089grt, eight in the South Atlantic and one in the southern Mozambique Channel.

The presence of a single commerce raider at large on the ocean trade routes posed a sufficient threat for the British and French navies to set up eight major battle groups (official British sources state ten, comprising 29 warships) to search for her, depriving merchant vessels elsewhere of essential protection. *Admiral Graf Spee's* seventh victim, the British freighter *Doric Star*, stopped and sunk on 3 December 1939 half-way between Sierra Leone and the Cape of Good Hope, managed to signal that she was being attacked by a 'pocket battleship'

On the morning of Wednesday 13 December 1939 *Admiral Graf Spee* was brought to battle off the coast of Uruguay by a small naval group consisting of the heavy cruiser HMS *Exeter* and the light cruisers HMS *Ajax* and HMNZS *Achilles*, the New Zealand vessel being the flagship of Rear-Admiral Harwood whose intuition based on the *Doric Star* signal had brought him to these waters. The weather was clear, with excellent visibility, the sea placid with a light swell, and there was a fresh breeze from the south-east. The three British cruisers were steering north-north-east in line ahead at 14kt. At 0614 smoke was sighted on the horizon to port and *Exeter* was detached to investigate. Two minutes later she reported: 'I think it is a pocket battleship.'

Admiral Graf Spee and the British group were approaching on a rapidly diminishing collision course. *Exeter*, with her 8in guns the most powerful ship of the three, altered course west, the two light cruisers with their 6in armament continuing north-east so as to close the range as quickly as possible, thus compelling the German commander to divide the fire of his two main turrets or leave one of the groups relatively unmolested.

At 0618 *Admiral Graf Spee* opened fire with her main armament and the two groups each received the attention of one turret. *Exeter* replied with her forward turrets at 0620 at 9.5nm range, all three turrets firing by 0623. Although *Ajax* and *Achilles* had opened a rapid and accurate fire at 0621 and 0623 respectively, Langsdorff concentrated both main turrets next on *Exeter* and straddled the heavy cruiser with the third salvo. Within a minute a whirlwind of splinters from a near-miss amidships killed men at the torpedo tubes, destroyed the command relay centre and peppered the funnels and searchlights; from the next salvo a 28cm shell put 'B' turret out of action, splinters killing or seriously wounding all present on the bridge bar the commander and two other men. While the ship was out

of control two further 28cm hits were sustained forward.

At 0630 Langsdorff again divided the fire of his main armament to drive off the light cruisers, which had worked up to 28kt and were uncomfortably close: his 15cm medium guns had concentrated on the two smaller vessels since the beginning of the battle but had managed only near-misses. At 0632 *Admiral Graf Spee* laid smoke and made a 150° turn which allowed a fan of torpedoes from *Exeter's* starboard tubes to pass harmlessly astern. At 0637 *Ajax* catapulted her ship's aircraft aloft. At 0638, as *Exeter* was turning to starboard to bring her portside torpedo tubes to bear, she received two 28cm hits which knocked out a main turret and started a fire between decks. She was now reduced to only two intact 8in guns. All her gyro-compasses had been destroyed and the commander was steering by a boat's compass; all communication in the ship was being performed by runners, a number of compartments were flooded and a dangerous fire was raging. She had a 7-degree list and was down by the head, although steaming at full speed.

At 0640 *Achilles* was hit near the bridge, the splinters killing four men in the gunnery control centre. At the same time *Admiral Graf Spee* laid smoke and headed west towards the coast, pursued at 31kt by the light cruisers whose north-west heading was masking their after turrets. *Exeter* followed as best she could on the German ship's port side. At 0656, when *Ajax* and *Achilles* altered to starboard away from the German ship to bring all turrets to bear, Langsdorff again laid smoke and turned away sharply, increasing the range to 8nm. By 0710 he was bearing down directly on *Exeter* to finish her off, but the fire of the two light cruisers was such that he was obliged to head off north-west and renew the concentration of his main turrets on them again, straddling *Ajax* with a 28cm salvo at 5.5nm range, although his 15cm secondary armament was continuing to maintain a ragged and inaccurate fire with no hits to report.

At 0720 *Admiral Graf Spee* was hit amidships and set on fire when subjected to heavy salvos from the light cruisers, but she laid another smoke screen and turned 130° to port to avoid torpedoes from *Ajax* loosed off at a range of 4.5nm. At 0725 *Ajax* was hit and lost the use of both after turrets; her aircraft, which had been sent up to spot the fall of shot, had also attempted to gain an impression of the damage aboard the German ship but was forced to circle just beyond the range of her Flak. *Exeter* had had to reduce speed and had fallen behind, occasionally firing rounds from her surviving turret, the gunnery officer directing fire from a searchlight platform. At 0730, when the

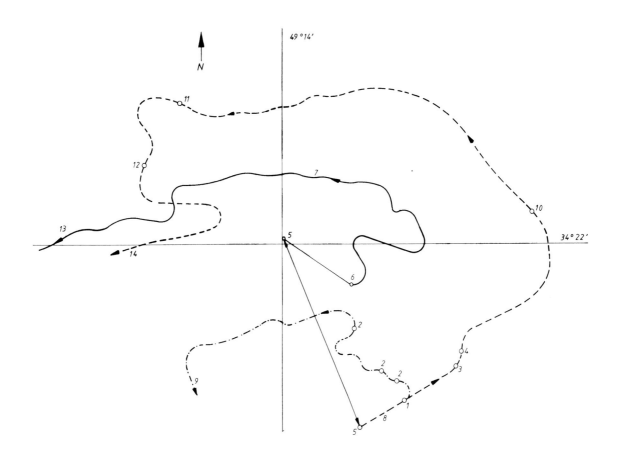

Above: Courses of the participants during the Battle of the River Plate

Key: (1) *Exeter* detached for recconnaissance. (2) Heavy hits on *Exeter*. (3) *Ajax* opens fire. (4) *Achilles* opens fire. (5) *Admiral Graf Spee* and Force G make initial sighting of each other almost simultaneously. (6) *Admiral Graf Spee* opens fire. (7) Course of *Admiral Graf Spee* with running alterations dictated by battle conditions. (8) Course of Force G with minor corrections during battle. (9) *Exeter* knocked out and retires in unbattleworthy condition to Falkland Islands. (10) Joint fire control aboard *Ajax* knocked out by hit. (11) *Ajax*'s 'X' and 'Y' turrets knocked out by hits. (12) *Ajax* hit and loses mainmast. (13) After disengaging, *Admiral Graf Spee* heads for Montevideo with enemy just beyond range. (14) Pursued by the two light cruisers.

last turret began to flood, *Exeter* was released and she retired to the south-east, taking no further part in the pursuit.

At 0728 *Ajax* and *Achilles* had turned west and at 0731 *Ajax*'s aircraft warned of torpedoes approaching well ahead of the cruiser's track. Harwood now headed directly for the German ship, even though *Ajax* had only three serviceable 6in guns, and the combined British fire forced Langsdorff to steer west, laying smoke to cover his zigzags. *Admiral Graf Spee* reappeared at 0736 on a bearing to the south-west so as to bring her main turrets to bear. The range was now only 4nm. Harwood, who had just been notified that his stock of shells was rapidly diminishing, decided to modify his tactics and merely shadow his opponent until nightfall, when he considered he would have a better chance of approaching the enemy ship unobserved for a gun and torpedo attack from close range. He was, of course, unaware that the German Panzerschiff was fitted with radar. At 0740, accordingly, the two British cruisers made smoke and bore east: while making the turn a hit destroyed *Ajax*'s mainmast and radio aerials, although a jury rig was soon erected. Langsdorff made no attempt to follow and persevered heading west at 22kt. After a short while the light cruisers took station on either quarter of the *Admiral Graf Spee* about fifteen miles astern.

At 1015 *Achilles* had approached within 11.5nm and was straddled by the second of two salvos from the

German main turret forward, which forced Harwood to fall back behind a curtain of smoke. At 1115 the German ship encountered the British freighter *Shakespeare* and ordered her to stop; a few minutes later Langsdorff signalled a request to the shadowers to pick up the survivors from a ship's boat adrift, this being a ruse to delay the pursuit. At 1915 *Admiral Graf Spee* fired a few salvos at a range of 13nm to reinforce the message, by which time it was already clear that she would probably be running into a neutral River Plate port to effect repairs. Salvos were exchanged at 2055, and the German ship fired desultory reminders at 2132, 2140 and 2143. At 0010 on the morning of 14 December 1939, the German 'pocket battleship' *Admiral Graf Spee* dropped anchor in the roadstead at Montevideo, Uruguay.

The balance sheet of damage and loss resulting from the Battle of the River Plate (all damage to the British ships having been inflicted by the German ship's main 28cm armament) was:

Exeter: 61 dead, 23 wounded. 'A' turret shut down due to flooded magazine, 'B' turret knocked out. Hits in forecastle, serious fire and flooding below decks. Bow-heavy trim, speed reduced, enforced retirement from battle.

Ajax: 7 dead and wounded. 'X' and 'Y' turrets plus one 6in gun on forward turret knocked out. Mainmast demolished.

Achilles: 4 dead. Superficial damage only.

Graf Spee: 36 dead, 60 wounded. Seventeen 6in hits causing minor damage, two 8in hits in non-vulnerable areas below armour deck, but oil purification and desalination plants destroyed, all kitchens wrecked. Ammunition stocks very low.

Essential repairs at Montevideo would have kept *Graf Spee* there for more than 72 hours, that being the maximum period allowed a belligerent warship to repair in a neutral port under international law. Cut off from home bases and having no hope of convincing this pro-British neutral state to bend the rules, the ship's captain saw himself caught in a trap.

The primary reason for scuttling the ship is often alleged to have been the belief that a superior British naval force consisting of the heavy cruiser HMS *Cumberland* and the aircraft carrier HMS *Ark Royal* had sealed off the estuary of the River Plate from seaward. No doubt these rumours, circulated by the British, contributed to the Ger-

mans' nervous state, which left no room for cool reflection, but, then as now, this remains propaganda. The crucial factor for Langsdorff was *Altmark*. In order to effect repairs and replenish ammunition, he had to meet his supply ship in some remote and secret area of the South Atlantic. He was able to put to sea immediately, but what worried him was not the possibly imaginary large force he could not see, but the two light cruisers *Ajax* and *Achilles*, which he could, watching him from just outside territorial waters. He knew it would be impossible to shake off these two shadowers. What stopped him from making a run for it to the north? There was a 2m gash in the bow which was considered too large for the North Atlantic in mid-winter. It would have meant a reduction in speed, and there were three narrow straits to break through and little ammunition, even if he had ever managed to get rid of the two shadowers. The loss of the ship might have cost 1,200 lives, and Langsdorff, contrary to most of the officers, was not prepared to take the risk.

Thus the circumstances determined Langsdorff's decision for him. Once the wounded had been cared for and *Admiral Graf Spee*'s dead interred in Montevideo with full military honours before a huge following – there was, and still is, a large German colony in Uruguay – Langsdorff put out in the Panzerschiff for the last time with a skeleton crew aboard at about 1830 on 17 December. His ship passed slowly through the dredged channel and turned her bows to face west before coming to a stop in a position in shallow water about 6nm south-west of the port. Detonators were fitted to scuttling charges which had been placed aboard earlier, and the crew members were transferred from the warship to the Argentinian tug *Colossus*. At about 2055 massive explosions rocked the hull, which was soon shrouded in flame and smoke from stem to stern. The explosions blew great holes in the hull and *Admiral Graf Spee* settled quickly on an even keel. The final act was watched by a huge crowd ashore and by the two British light cruisers waiting offshore, outside the territorial limits.

This was the first loss of a large Kriegsmarine warship. A fighting vessel of this size and power was irreplaceable at that time of the war. The ship's company were highly qualified career professionals and 50 per cent of them accepted internment for the duration, the remainder returning to the Reich within a year to resume naval service. Once his crew had been accepted by Buenos Aires, Kapitän zur See Langsdorff elected to commit suicide on 20 December 1939 and in a sense went down with his ship. His grave is to be found in the German Cemetery in Buenos

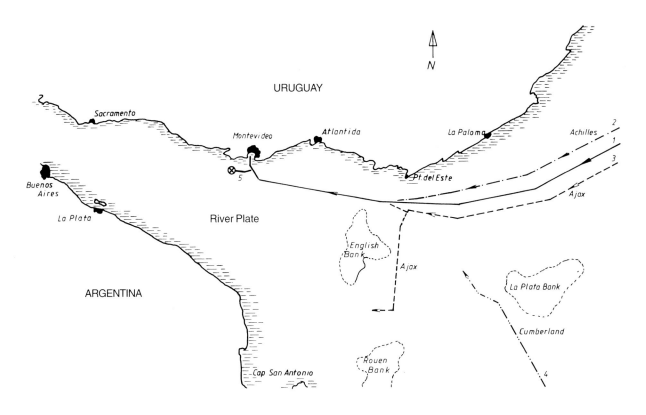

Above: The naval battle in the estuary of the River Plate, 13 December 1939

Key: (1) Approach course to Montevideo of *Admiral Graf Spee*. (2) Pursuit course of *Achilles*. (3) Pursuit course of *Ajax*. (4) Distant approach course of heavy cruiser HMS *Cumberland*. (5) *Admiral Graf Spee* moves into roadstead to scuttle, 17.12.1939. X = Present position of wreck.

Aires. The wreck of his ship is still visible from the air in certain conditions of light.

Reflections on the Loss of *Admiral Graf Spee*

The origin and outcome of the Battle of the River Plate lay in a chain of coincidences and errors of judgement. On 7 December 1939 charts had been found aboard the steamer *Streonshalh* which indicated off the River Plate an assembly area for merchant shipping. Langsdorff decided to head for it. The B-Dienst detected no enemy warship signals traffic, and it was thought that any opposition would be limited to a few AMCs. After the successful conclusion of the operation, it was planned that his ship would return to Germany, passing Iceland at the time of the January or February new moon, depending upon whether or not she had had to fight through the Natal–Freetown Narrows.

Was the battle and the subsequent loss of the ship avoidable? It had been drummed into the 'pocket battleship' crews that their ships were the best in the world.

One or two direct hits with their 28cm guns would put any cruiser afloat out of action – and they believed it. To what extent it was true the Battle of the River Plate was to show. All officers knew that the primary purpose of the commerce raider was to tie down enemy naval forces, and this was more important than tonnage sunk, but tonnage sunk is tangible and the crew suffered from a form of 'Emden Syndrome'. Langsdorff's operational orders stated: 'Avoid battle with warship(s) unless attacked . . .' *Admiral Graf Spee* sighted enemy masts a full ten minutes before the British saw his smoke, but at first they were not recognised as those of warships. The diesels of the German ship would have been at maximum speed up to an hour earlier than the British steam turbines could achieve, but, in warm seas and with four months' fouling below the waterline, the German ship was capable of 25kt maximum. For this reason, and also 'because he feared he would not be able to shake off the light cruisers', Langsdorff decided not to turn away.

Of the four ships involved, his main armament had the greatest range, but he compromised this advantage and elected to fight at short range for greater hitting power. This was possibly influenced by his relatively short stock of ammunition. It is not clear precisely when *Exeter* was identified: *Admiral Graf Spee*'s vertical armour was vulnerable to the heavy cruiser's 8in shells even at a range of 26.5km, and fortunately for Langsdorff the two hits received were not decisive. He must also have been slightly uncomfortable in the knowledge that his decks – and two-thirds of all hits at long range struck the deck – had a maximum 40mm armour protection and that 6in shells fired from 19km would penetrate them.

The Senior Gunnery Officer directed both the main and the secondary armament centrally. Against *Exeter* he used the wrong ammunition – explosive shells with fuse caps. He had his work cut out by the repeated changes of target for the main turrets, but even when the spotter for the 15cm battery was reporting nothing but misses he did not relinquish direction of the secondary armament to the responsible officer, the No 3 Gunnery Officer. The absolute priority was to sink *Exeter*. Everybody realised that. But Langsdorff forgot the principle 'Keep hitting your enemy until he goes down.'

Contrary to standing orders, during the battle Langsdorff was directing his ship from the foretop instead of the armoured control centre because the latter had insufficient command relay equipment. In the foretop he received a head wound, and when the First Officer was summoned from the damage control centre he took four minutes to arrive, during which time the ship was not under command. When eventually he got there the captain was still dazed and ordered him back to damage control. Obviously, this was a dangerous situation in the middle of a naval battle.

Langsdorff had been given command of *Admiral Graf Spee* in 1938 because as a career torpedo-boat man he needed sea-time as the commander of a heavy unit to qualify for promotion to Admiral. He was not a man who favoured decision-making alone but set store by teamwork, always making his decisions after detailed discussions with his two leading Navigation Officers, ADCs and the Chief Engineer. The First Officer was seldom consulted: before his appointment he had been in charge of NCO training at Friedrichsort and his tactical thinking was not rated very highly. When some thought had to be given to possible escape routes, hiding out in the Indian Ocean or making for Japan were both mulled over, but the ADCs advised against the latter for political reasons. The commander took a vote from a consensus of his officers and Buenos Aires was favoured as the neutral port of refuge. In a later conference Langsdorff abandoned his custom and discussed the River Plate only with his No 2 Navigation Officer, who knew the waters from his service in the merchant marine. This officer warned against the shallows on the Argentinian side as the cooling plant might clog with sand and advised Montevideo. The ADCs were only consulted on the naval and political regulations involved in making for a neutral port. Much later – in Buenos Aires – Argentine naval officers expressed surprise that nobody had considered putting in at the well-appointed naval base at Bahía Blanca, where the British would have had great difficulty in influencing the decision process in Argentina.

On the day of the scuttling an enormous state of confusion must have reigned. Not even the highly secret radar equipment was fully destroyed and the mattress aerial was left on the foretop. Visits to the wreck were made by British experts in December 1939 to inspect the welding of the Wotan armour and aluminium components and in March 1940 for a look at the radar.

Logistics

In 1930 the US Naval War Academy under Admiral Lansing developed the so-called 'N-Square Law' which propounded the principles for determining the stronger side in a battle between ships of the same class. This can be applied to the Battle of the River Plate if *Admiral Graf Spee* is held to be a cruiser, and in that case the odds against her were 9:1. The dictum that a *Deutschland* class Panzerschiff was invulnerable because she could 'outrun any ship sufficiently powerful to sink her or outgun any ship fast enough to catch her' is only true against a single opponent.

Admiral Graf Spee's broadside (main and secondary armament) was:

$$6 \times 300 \text{ plus } 8 \times 45.5 = 1800 \text{ plus } 364 = 2{,}164 \text{kg}$$

The combined broadside of the British ships was:

$$\textit{Exeter } 6 \times 116.1 \text{ plus } \textit{Ajax/Achilles } 16 \times 50.8 = 1{,}509.4 \text{kg}$$

– an advantage for the German ship, but when adjusted for the rate of fire:

$$\textit{Admiral Graf Spee } 6 \times 300 \times 2 \text{ rds/min plus } 8 \times 45.5 \times 4 \text{ rds/min} = 44 \text{ rds/min total } 5{,}056 \text{kg}.$$

Above: Panzerschiff 'C' under construction at Wilhelms-haven, Slip 1: a view across the roof of the boilermaking shop. In the yard basin (top right) is the light cruiser *Leipzig*.
Right: The launch of *Admiral Graf Spee*, 30 June 1934.

Exeter/Ajax/Achilles 6 × 116.1 × 4 rds/min plus 16 × 50.8 × 6 rds/min = 120 rds/min total 7,663.2kg.

– an advantage for the British ships.

When further adjusted for the *Admiral Graf Spee* having to divide her fire among three opponents her broadside per minute is 1,685kg, an inferiority of 8:1. (Her 10.5cm guns are discounted as not significant.)

The gunnery of all four ships was poor, having regard to the excellent weather conditions. Both sides would normally expect a 4 per cent hit rate. *Ajax/Achilles* achieved 4.82 per cent, *Exeter* 2.66 and *Admiral Graf Spee* 3.48. (The gunnery of the German ship was complicated by frequent changes of target, and latterly *Exeter* was firing at a disadvantage on account of the damage inflicted on her.) The two light cruisers had a common fire control and their shooting could not be distinguished. A decisive factor of the battle may have been the inaccuracy of the German 15cm guns, the hit rate of which was 0 per cent.

Left: Another view of the hull sliding sternwards into the fitting-out basin, cheered by the countless thousands of onlookers who always turned out for this type of occasion.

Above: The name board exposed at the completion of the launching ceremony.
Below: The hull is moved by tugs to the fitting-out quay.

Above: *Admiral Graf Spee* at berth B5, a fitting-out quay between the stocks and Drydock IV.

Below: A port-side view of the hull. On the slipway new staging has been erected, probably for building work on the new battlecruiser *Scharnhorst*. The two main 28cm turrets and parts of the superstructure deck have been installed aboard the Panzerschiff.

Right, upper: The funnel mantle being manoeuvred by crane prior to lowering over the two exhaust tubes with their noise suppressors. The hull is riding high in the water, exposing the belt armour and bulging trim tanks amidships.

Right, lower: *Admiral Graf Spee* in the Jade on 22 February 1936, heading for Wilhelmshaven after trials; she had entered service the previous month. The semaphore flags at the pole mast abaft the foretop notify Lock III signal station of her intention to enter.

Above: A photograph taken on the same day as the previous exposure, looking aft from the icy foredeck.
Below: *Admiral Graf Spee* at her moorings in Kieler Förde with propeller guards extended and lively boat traffic at the foot of an accommodation ladder. The three barrels of 'B' turret ('Gneisenau') are slightly elevated.

Above: Alongside wooden mooring stages at Swinemünde, *Admiral Graf Spee* as Fleet flagship, with an admiral's pennant at the foretop pole mast.

Below: A midships view shows how the pole mast extended almost to the superstructure deck – twice the length of the fixture aboard *Admiral Scheer*. On the catapult is He 60 floatplane '60+F91'.

Above: *Admiral Graf Spee* in Norwegian waters, early July 1938.

Below: At Kiel, with both forward mooring poles extended. Astern of the communication boat is a refuse barge: care was taken not to litter the harbour with ship's rubbish.

Right: *Admiral Graf Spee*'s bridge superstructure as seen in 1937. The armoured hood of 'A' turret rangefinder can just be seen at right, behind which is the 7m rangefinder of the forward command centre and, slightly above this, the AA fire control centre. On the pagoda-like tower below the 'Coronel' plaque (commemorating the German naval victory in 1914) is the admiral's bridge and, one deck lower, the bridge command platform. Above the plaque are two searchlight platforms (later replaced by a single platform on the forward face); above these is the octagonal foretop with the 10.5cm rangefinder of the main gunnery control centre. Atop the dome is a windspeed measuring device; forward of the foretop are direction-finding loops.

Above: *Admiral Graf Spee* from astern, a ship's boat suspended from the hook of both shipboard cranes and with an accommodation ladder let down.

Right: A lifejacketed crewman unstowing the oars of the 10-man cutter during the setting-down manoeuvre.

Below: Securing at a buoy with cutter assistance.

Above: The People's Navy Week, Kieler Förde, May 1936. Commemoration Day for the Battle of Jutland was arranged to coincide with the unveiling by Hitler of the Naval Memorial at Laboe. Seen here at moorings are *Admiral Graf Spee*, with the pennant of the Naval C-in-C hoisted at the foretop, and, beyond her, *Admiral Scheer*. In the background is the new State yacht *Grille*.

Right, upper: *Admiral Graf Spee*'s shipboard band. As Fleet flagship the band would be augmented by musician personnel from the Fleet Staff: the two ceremonial Obergefreiter (Leading Seaman) trumpeters and the trombonist are identified as members of the Fleet Staff by the admiral's pennant patch worn on the left sleeve above the lyre insignia.

Right, lower: *Admiral Graf Spee* off the port quarter of her sister-ship *Deutschland* during a gunnery exercise. These were held very frequently, either alone or in formation, or as the climax to Fleet manoeuvres.

Above: *Admiral Graf Spee*'s crew parade during the Naval Review by the German Chancellor, 29 May 1936. The German tradition is for the flagship to lead the units of the Fleet in line astern past the State yacht.

Below: Hitler's arrival at Kiel on 28 May 1936 was marked by the usual 21-gun salute fired by all naval vessels in the harbour. Seen here (from left to right) are *Admiral Graf Spee*, *Admiral Scheer*, *Deutschland* and two light cruisers.

Top: Each night during People's Navy Week the skies were illuminated by a great display of searchlights.

Left: The German Naval Cenotaph was conceived by Wilhelm Lammertz, a former Senior NCO in the Imperial Navy. His idea found little interest in official circles but received much support from dignitaries such as the naval deacon Ronneberger, the retired Admiral Scheer and the Navy League. The design was the work of the Düsseldorf architect Professor Munzer and the construction was financed by voluntary contributions. The monument, which stands at the entrance to Kieler Förde, can be seen from far offshore and is now dedicated to all seafarers lost at sea. Today all warships honour the dead by dipping their ensigns in passing.

Above: The dedication of the monument. Front row from left: Admiral Raeder, C-in-C Navy; Hitler; Feldmarschall von Blomberg, Reich War Minister; Admiral Albrecht, Commanding Admiral Baltic; and Kapitän zur See Mewis, Naval Commander Kiel.

Left, top: The German leader prepares to be piped aboard the Fleet flagship *Admiral Graf Spee* at Kiel in the summer of 1936. The admiral's barge bearing Hitler (third from left) is at the foot of the accommodation ladder. Divisions of the ship's company are mustered on the quarterdeck, the honour guard on the upper deck has presented arms and drummer and bugler await their great moment.

Left, centre: *Admiral Graf Spee* adorned with lights on a night during People's Navy Week.

Left, bottom: The daily routine for the Commander and First Officer included tasting the men's food. Fregattenkapitän Kienast looks on as Kapitän zur See Warzecha samples the midday meal brought from the galley by a runner.

Right, upper: The crew of *Admiral Graf Spee* parade along the port rail during the welcoming home ceremonies for the returning Legion Kondor veterans at Hamburg, May 1939.

Right, lower: A high point in the career of *Admiral Graf Spee* was her participation at Spithead in the international celebrations to mark the Coronation of King George VI. She was selected to represent the Third Reich as the most modern heavy unit of the Kriegsmarine. Here, on her arrival at the anchorage, she fires a salute from an 8.8cm gun amidships.

Left: Four photographs of *Admiral Graf Spee* at anchor at Spithead, surrounded by warships of all nations. Closest to her (top left) are the battlecruiser HMS *Hood* and a battleship of the *Royal Sovereign* class. As a hybrid the German ship attracted special interest from foreign navies and was always a subject for the photographers. Note the Reich battle ensign at the foretop – customary on all foreign visits.

Above, left and right: *Admiral Graf Spee*'s officers in ceremonial dress – frock coats, cocked hats, sabres, epaulettes and medals. The photograph on the left shows Kapitän zur See Patzig; that on the right shows the officer corps of the German ship (at the far left is a British naval liaison officer).

Right, upper: The British method of review was for the Royal yacht bearing the monarch to steam past the ranks of anchored warships. Here the crew of *Admiral Graf Spee* line the starboard rail. In the background is the battleship *Queen Elizabeth*.

Right, lower: A photograph taken from *Admiral Graf Spee*'s bridge, looking over the foredeck and showing crew members lining the forecastle rails. A motor torpedo-boat is seen crossing between the German vessel's bow and the stern of the Royal yacht *Victoria and Albert*.

Left, top: In June 1937 an American battleship division consisting of the USS *Wyoming* (BB22), *Arkansas* (BB33) and *New York* (BB34) visited Kiel. The photograph shows the Fleet C-in-C, Admiral Carls, being received aboard the flagship *New York*. In the background are *Admiral Graf Spee* and, nearer the camera, one of the numerous passenger ferries of the Förde.

Left, centre: The ship's band of *Admiral Graf Spee* at rehearsal during one of the vessel's Spanish tours of duty.

Left, bottom: Ships that pass . . . : the Italian passenger liner *Rex*.

Right, upper: The contents of cases and crates stacked on the foredeck are turned out for stowing and – probably strictly against regulations – the unwanted packaging is cast over the side.

Right, lower: A view from the bridge of off-watch personnel taking the sun on the forecastle. Notice how 'A' turret has been painted with recognition stripes in the national colours.

Left: During patrols and exercises with other Kriegsmarine units in Spanish waters collisions occurred from time to time. Seen on this page are photographs depicting the aftermath of one such collision, between *Admiral Graf Spee* and *U 35* (Kapitänleutnant Werner Lott) on 17 March 1938. The Panzerschiff's damaged port propeller is seen, as is *U 35* returning home surfaced for repairs. The other photographs show various aspects of the U-boat's damaged conning tower and smashed forecasing and were used later for propaganda purposes ('One of our U-boats returns safely to port after a fierce Atlantic convoy battle').

Above: *Admiral Graf Spee* on 19 June 1938 at anchor in Wilhelmshaven Roads, a communication boat in attendance at an extended mooring pole forward.

Below: On 31 October 1938 Fleet C-in-C Admiral Carls was relieved and he hauled down his pennant aboard *Admiral Graf Spee*. In accordance with tradition he was rowed off in a cutter manned by staff officers while the crews of all units in harbour paraded on board ship. At the cutter's bows is the admiral's pennant, at the stern the Reich battle flag – which was only hoisted in a ship's boat when an officer was aboard.

Left, upper: During Admiral Carls's departure individual ships also fired a salute, and the camera has caught the smoke from *Leipzig*'s round just forward of *Admiral Graf Spee*'s bow. This and the previous photograph show good detail following the ship's refit: on the bridge superstructure forward are two paravanes for streaming the bow anti-mine gear, and the two searchlights either side of the battle-mast have been unshipped and replaced by a single searchlight on a platform forward.

Left, lower: The last major Kriegsmarine exercise in foreign waters before the outbreak of war was held in May 1939 off the Spanish mainland and the Canaries. This photograph shows some of the units at the Spanish North African port of Ceuta, opposite Gibraltar. In the foreground is the 10,000-ton naval oiler *Altmark* (Kapitän Dau), which would supply *Admiral Graf Spee* during her South Atlantic commerce-raiding cruise in late 1939, the submarines *U 51* (Heinicke), *U 47* (Prien) and *U 45* (Gelhaar) and, astern, *Admiral Scheer* and the U-boat tender *Erwin Wassner*.

Right: *Admiral Graf Spee*'s bridge superstructure in 1939. Notice, at the foretop, the revolving cupola of the 10.5cm main rangefinder, on which a mattress-type aerial for the FuMG 39(go) – later FuMO 22 – radar has been mounted and concealed beneath a canvas cover.

Left, upper: Late August 1939: *Admiral Graf Spee* heads for her South Atlantic waiting position. 'A' turret is trained to starboard on account of the heavy seas being shipped over the forecastle.

Left, lower: 3 September 1939: the crew parades aft to receive notification of the British and French declaration of war on Germany.

Right, upper: The naval oiler *Altmark* refuelled *Admiral Graf Spee* on several occasions and relieved her of her Merchant Navy prisoners. Here the warship takes on board the tanker's hawser and oil hose prior to a refuelling tow.

Right, lower: During the waiting period in the South Atlantic an intensive schedule of training and exercises was maintained aboard *Admiral Graf Spee*. Here the anti-gas squad poses for the camera.

Right, top and centre: The German raider's first victim, the 5,051brt freighter *Clement*, was spotted by *Admiral Graf Spee*'s floatplane on 30 September 1939. The British ship had a cargo of oil, coal and mixed goods. She was sunk with a few rounds from the main armament, scuttling charges and a torpedo having failed to sink her. The crew made the nearby coast of Pernambuco in three lifeboats. No loss of life was occasioned by *Admiral Graf Spee* during her cruise.

Below: The seventh and largest of *Admiral Graf Spee*'s victims was the 10,086brt refrigerator ship *Doric Star*, en route from Cape Town to Freetown for the UK with 8,000 tons of food-stuffs and wool, sunk on 3 December 1939 off the coast of South-West Africa by gunfire after scuttling charges had proved ineffective. The German ship opened fire at very long range, which gave the *Doric Star* time to send a series of wireless messages – which were instrumental in having the *Admiral Graf Spee* brought to battle ten days later.

Above: A ruse intended to deceive prisoners coming aboard was a nameplate announcing the ship as the *Deutschland* – although the quotation marks may have aroused suspicions amongst keener observers!

Below: Attempts were made to deceive enemy vessels by altering the outline of the Panzerschiff. This photograph shows a fake funnel abaft the catapult and a dummy superfiring turret forward of the battle-mast. The materials used for these devices were usually wood, canvas and paint.

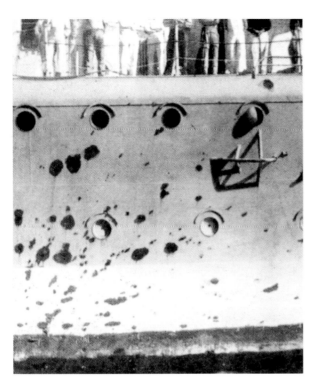

Opposite page: After a relatively short but initially successful commerce raiding interlude in the South Atlantic and Indian Ocean (50,089brt sunk), *Admiral Graf Spee* was intercepted by British cruisers about 150 miles off the estuary of the River Plate. After the action was broken off, Kapitän zur See Langsdorff elected to repair the worst of his ship's battle damage in the neutral port of Montevideo – a fateful decision which spelt doom for his ship since the port proved to be a trap. The photographs show shell damage to the German Panzerschiff, including her wrecked shipboard aircraft. A shell passed through the battle-mast at the level of the searchlight platform.

Top left: An 8in shell passed through the coaming of the admiral's bridge.

Top right: Temporary repairs to patch over a 6in hit in the port forecastle.

Above left: The ruins of the shipboard Arado 196 floatplane.

Left and above right: At Montevideo *Admiral Graf Spee*'s dead were laid out on the forecastle deck prior to being encased in coffins. The latter, some draped with the Reich battle ensign, were arranged in rows with an honour guard.

This page: The funeral ceremony for *Admiral Graf Spee*'s 36 fallen. There was a large colony of German settlers in Uruguay, and many attended as mourners. German clergymen give the Hitler salute, Kapitän zur See Langsdorff the naval salute. Below left is seen the Commander's final farewell at the graveside.

Opposite page, upper: After the decision had been taken to scuttle the Panzerschiff, the ship's company disembarked, leaving behind only the essential technicians, explosives personnel and a skeleton crew to remove the ship to the seaward position where she was to be sunk. Here kitbags and other personal belongings are loaded aboard lighters alongside the doomed warship.

Opposite page, lower: *Admiral Graf Spee* in the roadstead at Montevideo wearing a false bow wave, the purpose of which was to deceive enemy rangefinder operators as to her speed.

This page: *Admiral Graf Spee* sets out on her last short voyage, waved off by thousands of unsuspecting onlookers. At the limits of Uruguayan territorial waters the scuttling charges are fused and a few hours later massive blasts and a huge cloud tell their own story. The skeleton crew returns to Montevideo aboard the Argentine tug *Colossus*.

Above: The burning wreck of *Admiral Graf Spee*, torn apart by numerous explosions. This view is amidships, looking from the port side.

Below: The midships section, with the collapsed funnel evident. The black smoke indicates raging fires within the ship's hull. These photographs were taken eight days after the scuttling.

This spread: Comprehensive destruction: the burning wreck from the air. The battle-mast shows the undamaged and classified radar aerial at the foretop. Until the River Plate action the British Admiralty was unaware that Germany had developed radar for gunnery-ranging purposes.

Above and left, upper: The wreck of *Admiral Graf Spee* showing the battle-mast and displaced funnel.

Left, lower: The wreck at a distance, upright but slowly settling, February 1940.

Above left: Kapitän zur See Langsdorff surrounded by his men in Argentine internment. He gave no hint that he saw the need to take his own life as a matter of honour.

Above right: After having satisfied himself as to the safety of all surviving crew members, Langsdorff shot himself in the head with his service pistol. Here officers from *Admiral Graf Spee* carry his coffin to the graveside in the small German cemetery at Buenos Aires. Many of the German expatriate community considered this an event at which to express their political solidarity.

Above, left and right: The commander's burial. The Argentine authorities permitted the ship's company, though interned, to assemble in full naval dress for the final muster.

Below: This ornate sailor's chest, painstakingly crafted by crew members in internment, was intended as a gift for the commander's family. About half the crew managed to return to Germany during the war. The remainder settled in Argentina, where they established the small settlement of Villa Belgrano in the province of Cordoba.

This page: *Admiral Graf Spee*'s principal opponent in the River Plate battle was the heavy cruiser *Exeter*. These four photographs illustrate damage sustained by the British ship: to 'A' and 'B' 8in turrets (above), and to the superstructure and hull (below).

Conclusions

With the construction of the first *Deutschland* class 'pocket battleship', the German Navy had broken new ground. In respect of the Versailles Treaty as amended by the 1922 Washington Agreement, German naval architects had apparently put a quart into a pint pot. It is the German contention that if there were a breach of the 10,000-ton displacement limit for cruisers, it was in the cause of more protection and not hitting power. *Deutschland* thrust the small Reichsmarine into the spotlight and aroused the political interest of the major naval powers.

On 8 January 1930 the *Naval and Military Record* remarked that, both strategically and tactically, the ship presented a factor impossible to ignore: Germany had proved to the world that major increases in battleship size were superfluous and bore no relationship to calculations of battle effectiveness, and on 22 January, in the same periodical, Sir Herbert Russell observed that the new type seemed to him to be the battleship of the future, combining the qualities of a battleship with those of a cruiser. By abandoning much conservative tradition out of sheer necessity, German warship designers had changed naval strategy: the Panzerschiffe soon underpinned oceanic commerce-raiding policy.

After *Deutschland* had berthed on 19 April 1935 following her long Atlantic voyage, Konteradmiral Carls reported to Fleet Command that 'the ship has cruised 12,286 nautical miles in almost exactly 32 days. This corresponds to an average of 384 nautical miles per day at an average speed of 16 knots . . . since 20 hours for various stoppages has not been deducted, the averages are actually understated . . . as regards her sea-keeping qualities, propulsion machinery and suitability for tropical waters the ship proved excellent throughout the cruise . . . in my opinion the voyage has proved comprehensively the value and suitability of the ship and its class for extended cruiser operations . . .'

Deutschland's commander, Kapitän zur See Hermann von Fischel, reported on 18 June 1935: 'During the five-week long Atlantic cruise of March/April 1935, as on earlier voyages, Panzerschiff *Deutschland* has proved an outstanding sea boat. Even in the three-day unbroken period of heavy weather with wind strengths from Force 8 to 10 and driving diagonally into a corresponding seaway and Atlantic swell, it was still possible to maintain a speed of 15 knots without danger . . . in heavy seas and swell from broadside, full speed could be maintained with rolls to a maximum of 24 degrees . . . stationary across the swell the ship rode with only light rolling movements . . . proceeding into heavy seas some damage was sustained by "A" turret, and as the foreship rose water was scooped as far aft as the upper deck amidships, such that the addition of a breakwater on the forecastle and deflectors forward of "A" turret is desirable . . . The ship spent twenty days in tropical waters. The motor drive was in no way affected adversely by the higher temperatures . . . one can summarise by saying that the engine plant has proved itself in all respects and seems especially well suited for the longer type of cruiser voyage . . .'

In general, however, all reports tended to play down deficiencies and weaknesses.

Hull and Armour Protection

The *Deutschland* class hybrid was an imaginative development in warship design resulting directly from the displacement restrictions imposed by the Treaty of Versailles. The ships were superior in fire power to any cruiser. At 10,000 tons' displacement, *Deutschland* was a cruiser by definition but carried the armament of a capital ship, the armour being thin to keep her within the limit. Because the range of her guns, or the speed of the ship, could hold a faster or more powerful adversary, respectively, at a safe distance, a degree of armour thickness had been sacrificed in the interests of saving weight. Her deck armour was weak, but in this *Deutschland* did not differ from the ships of other navies: at the time designers had still not taken into account how dangerous would become the threat from the air. The air attack on *Deutschland* at Ibiza in 1937 may have driven this point home, but by then it was too late to strengthen the armour as the ship had been finely built to the weight margins. Initial moves towards more protection in this respect could be made with *Admiral Scheer* and *Admiral Graf Spee*, where the displacement was greater.

In 1930 the Heinrich Hertz Institute was given the task by the Reichsmarine of conducting extensive tests into the effects of vibration resulting from diesel propulsion aboard warships, and these were carried out between 1931 and 1934. The research activity investigated principally how the sensitive optics and trigonometrical computing equipment in the fire control centres, plus the welding in the ship's hull, reacted to vibrational stresses.

Deutschland and the gunnery training ship *Bremse* were the first large warships to have exclusively diesel propulsion. The motors were double-acting two-stroke MAN marine diesels of uniquely light construction, a condition of manufacture having been a saving in weight even down to the foundations.

The tests showed that substantial vibration from the motors was felt throughout the ship and that this vibration was just as strong as that imparted by the propellers. The engine vibration had a frequency corresponding to the revolutions, while the exhaust discharge system had an audible frequency which was actually intolerable.

Worst affected were the rangefinders, which were unserviceable over a range of speeds, the operators experiencing fatigue at the optics after even short periods of observation; the gunnery, torpedo and searchlight optics reported similar but less extreme distress. At all these positions the vibration was occasionally so strong that it was impossible to obtain an image through the instrument. At certain speeds equipment installed in the battle-mast, and especially at the foretop, was unusable.

After the ships had been in commission for a short period, welded seams and the corners of the engine foundations burst and expanded so quickly that engine revolutions had to be strictly regulated to contain the damage. The overall picture, particularly with regard to the latter weakness, was at first so grave that diesel drive for warships began to be regarded as the wrong path in important policy circles. This was grist to the mill for conservatives advocating marine turbines, and the steam lobby experienced a major revival.

It is extremely difficult to eliminate vibration by modifications to a finished ship, even when the cause is clearly recognised, but, nevertheless, on existing diesel-driven units ways were generally found to reduce levels to tolerable limits. In *Deutschland* the motor chassis and foundations were strengthened; in the later ships of the class various compromise measures were introduced or levels accepted as an alternative to increasing engine weight and reducing propeller effectiveness or engine output. Aboard *Admiral Scheer* the foretop fire control centre

was unserviceable because of longitudinal and transverse vibration at certain propeller revolutions. This problem was resolved by devising an independent suspension for the armoured foretop in parallel with a liquid absorbent for the horizontal vibration, which achieved a 90 per cent reduction in vibration levels.

Weapons and Fire Control Systems

For their size the Panzerschiffe were over-armed. This fault had its origins in the Versailles Treaty, which stipulated that a new battleship had to be a replacement for an existing obsolete unit, but it was impossible for Germany to construct a modern, combat-worthy battleship within the tonnage limitations. The Treaty provided for a cruiser tonnage limit of 10,000 tonnes without specifying a maximum armament, and the 1922 Washington Agreement stated that the maximum displacement for a cruiser was 10,000 long tons but with a maximum 8in calibre. The German 'compromise' was not a cruiser within either definition, and so a new type of warship altogether, a Panzerschiff, presented as the legitimate replacement for the pre-dreadnought battleship *Braunschweig*, came into existence.

From a general point of view, the 28cm calibre was too large for the cruiser hull. Even the 15cm (5.9in) secondary armament was more suitable aboard a battleship than a cruiser. In retrospect, a multi-purpose battery would have been preferable to the medium guns and at least the heavy Flak, and not only on account of the savings in weight. However, no satisfactory multi-purpose weapon was available at the time. German industry remained subject to Allied supervision and control until the mid-1930s, and the major companies were in the French-occupied Ruhr. By the time the situation had been remedied much valuable time had been lost. Initially *Deutschland* was fitted with the obsolete 88 mm (3.5in) anti-aircraft weapon which had been standard in the First World War; this was not replaced by the more modern 10.5cm (4.1in) heavy AA gun until 1940. There were similar problems with the light Flak.

An acrimonious difference of opinion existed between the Engineering Branch of Naval High Command (OKM) and the Warship Gun Test Branch (AVKS) regarding the value of the Flak fire control system, and this had not been resolved even by the time the *Bismarck* class were in service.

Machinery

After initial defects in construction (not entirely the fault of the manufacturer) had been overcome in the first few years after commissioning, the engines proved themselves totally. Obviously the problems were worst in *Deutschland* and progressively less severe on board *Admiral Scheer* and *Admiral Graf Spee*. Sources opposed to the introduction of diesels in major fleet units made capital out of the defects and influenced the Reichsmarine to abandon the idea. The fourth and fifth Panzerschiffe, 'D' and 'E' (*Scharnhorst* and *Gneisenau*), were redesigned on the grounds of political necessity as battlecruisers and had steam turbine drive, as did the last German battleships *Bismarck* and *Tirpitz*.

Konteradmiral Fuchs wrote: 'In October 1935 I was made Departmental Head of A IV at the OKM. A IV dealt with matters of training and military questions in warship construction because all weapons specialists were attached to the department at the time. A I was responsible for warship construction, i.e. A I laid down the specific requirements for a ship type, from which, under the overall control of A IV, the so-called military requirements were worked out in collaboaration with K (Office of Naval Architecture). From these K and A IV drew up the design sketches. After these had been approved by the C-in-C of the Reichsmarine, K prepared the blueprints and supervised the building of the ship.

'Hitler was very interested in the Navy, particularly the technical side. As Raeder was usually unable to answer specific technical questions and had to find out the answer for himself first, I was given the task of speaking to Hitler on the subject of developments in warship construction two or three times each year. It always amazed me how much technical information Hitler managed to absorb, even if some of the connections were missing. He set aside a surprising amount of time for my lectures, and if it was delivered in the morning, I would then be invited to lunch. One day I was seated next to a high Party functionary who told me, "Herr Kapitän, it is easy for you with the Führer because he is at heart a naval officer who missed his calling." During these lectures Hitler would occasionally speak of his political intentions involving the Navy and as there was no propaganda point to be made I assume he was speaking of his real convictions. He said that the primary purpose of the Fleet must be to prevent a blockade of the German ports. Iron ore imports were of the greatest importance: when these were cut off in the Great War it had made a longer defence of Germany impossible. There could never be a question of the German [surface] Navy blockading enemy ports in the Atlantic theatre, and naval surface warfare would be limited to cruiser or merchant raider operations against the trade routes. For the

latter reason, equipping the Panzerschiffe had been an important decision in the reconstruction of the Fleet. The suggestion had come from Vizeadmiral Bauer.

'The tragedy in German warship construction was the return to high-pressure steam turbines for the large warships, although it was a satisfactory solution for smaller units in the coastal theatre. When I entered the OKM in October 1935 the decision had already been taken: high-pressure steam turbines for the battleships and heavy cruisers . . .

'The Panzerschiffe could range into the Indian Ocean, whereas steam-turbine drive limited a battleship or cruiser to the North Atlantic. Actually, the term 'range' is misleading. Apart from the distance they could cover without refuelling, the Panzerschiffe could just drift, knowing that if necessary they could work up almost immediately to full speed at the push of a button. Steam must be kept up in a turbine ship even if stopped, for cold turbines need two hours to reach maximum output. The difference between the types of drive in distant oceans is therefore much greater than mere range.'

Former Marineoberbaurat Ehrenburg once explained in a lecture: 'Diesel drive was common aboard small warships and universal on U-boats, and the merchant marine had adopted it long previously. When it was introduced aboard *Bremse* and *Deutschland*, ships of a size which had never previously been equipped with it, it aroused a determined resistance in naval engineering circles, who succeeded initially in having it rejected for future new construction . . . the development of new boilers types had led to the production of very high-pressure hot steam (60 to 70 atmospheres) with superheating to 470° in shipboard drive . . . in a number of respects the diesel had been equalled or overhauled for the time being . . . but in terms of thermal effectiveness the diesel has a lead of 37 per cent and with use of exhaust gases even 40 per cent . . .'

The advantages of low fuel consumption, self-contained individual sets of motor, smaller openings in the armour deck as a result of faster exhaust expulsion, enclosed air intakes for combustion and so on were factors of too great importance in warship construction to be easily dismissed, even if the questions of vibration and noise remained problematical. The principal disadvantages of marine turbines were the uneconomic use of space, the over-complicated nature of the units, the difficulties of maintenance and repair, the time needed to build up steam and the high fuel consumption, especially when cruising – which was particularly disadvantageous since it limited range so severely as to make even North Atlantic operations questionable. On the other hand, many claimed advantages for diesel over steam had been refuted in practice. On balance there seemed nothing to choose between them, and, in the absence of a positive reason for adopting exclusively diesel drive, the decision to continue with the steam turbine for the large units on the stocks practically made itself.

Years of polemic for and against ensued, but not until 1938 did the question suddenly become topical again, and the majority were in favour of diesel. But the Germany Navy had missed the bus. Years which could have been devoted to the development of an improved diesel were lost. MAN-Diesel had continued the work privately, but they lacked the active support of the Kriegsmarine, which had given the nod to steam.

Discussions regarding the correct choice began before 1933. On 17 November of that year Admiral Raeder wrote to all four Departmental Heads requesting comprehensive reports on the pros and cons of a range of considerations. The Head of the General Naval Office summarised the various opinions: 'The question of military use comes down firmly in favour of the turbine. If the construction of a high-pressure steam turbine suitable to the technical requirements is now feasible, I support the installation on the grounds of the military application . . .'

After the war, Grossadmiral Raeder explained: 'My decision in favour of the high-pressure steam turbine was temporary until such time as a diesel type became available suitable to the greater demands and technical requirements made of it.' However in a letter dated 4 July 1940 acknowleging his gratitude to the firm of MAN-Diesel, he stated that '. . . the engines of Admiral Graf Spee had been adequate to all tasks required of them throughout the entire period of the South Atlantic operation'. An officer of the cruiser stated to the author in a private letter that 'the Spee was an absolutely first-class ship. MAN-Diesel can pride themselves on it. After four months at sea and despite heavy bottom fouling, the ship managed a half-knot more than the designed speed throughout the River Plate battle . . .'

Final Observations

On the whole the Panzerschiffe were political ships. They were to bring Germany political respectability within international naval treaties and win allies. In war, their task would be to safeguard the seaway to East Prussia and protect the Baltic entrances and the North Sea approaches. In 1929, when the great range of these ships was realised, grander prospects emerged for their deployment – attacks on French shipping off West African ports, in the Mediterranean and, if the political situation permitted, also off North Africa.

Germany had no overseas naval bases – perhaps her most significant disadvantage in comparison to the major sea powers – and when the idea of using the Panzerschiffe as commerce raiders on the world's oceans was first conceived (probably in the summer of 1934 after Deutschland had completed her South Atlantic voyage) the need for purpose-built supply ships was realised. Sound refuelling methods had to be established, and extensive investigations were made using chartered tankers during the operations in Spanish waters. The experience gained was applied to the Altmark class naval oilers then under construction.

In the event, the Panzerschiffe were used as makeweights in the tonnage war, and only Admiral Scheer, with an adroit commander, skilful handling by the SKL (Naval Warfare Directorate) and a great deal of luck, paid a major dividend.

Warfare against merchant shipping is the business of light cruisers. The Royal and US Navies themselves had found the 20.3cm (8in) battery too ponderous for the task. Instead of the heavy cruiser types with which it equipped itself, the German Navy might have been better served by a class of well-armoured, fast, diesel-driven light cruisers of optimum armament for commerce-raiding purposes. This was not given consideration.

The German Fleet could never have been of a size to challenge Britain's for control of the seas, and the question must be asked whether there was any logic in building ships of heavy cruiser size and above. They were too big for duties in the German Bight and adjacent areas, the era of the great sea battle being past, and they were only latterly of any use in the Baltic.

What the German Navy lacked was overseas bases and safe refuelling at sea far from home. The loss of seven out of eight supply ships stationed in mid-Atlantic for the Bismarck adventure in May 1941 after the enemy had seized the 'Enigma' coding machine and broken the 'Ultra' code drove this point home.

Bibliography

BOOKS

Assmann, Kurt, *Deutsche Seestrategie in zwei Weltkriegen*, Heidelberg, 1957
Baeuerlein, Hans, *Chronik Admiral Scheer*, 1982
———, *Kreuzer Admiral Scheer*, 1988
Bekker, Cajus, *Ostsee, deutsches Schicksal 1944/45*, Oldenburg, 1959
Bennett, Geoffrey, *Coronel and the Falklands*, London/New York, 1962
———, *Naval Battles of World War Two*, London/New York, 1976
———, *The Battle of Jutland*, London, 1964
Bensel, Rolf, *Die deutsche Flottenpolitik von 1933–1939*, Berlin, 1958
Bidlingmaier, Gerhard, *Einsatz der schweren Kriegsmarineeinheiten im ozeanischen Zufuhrkrieg*, Neckargemünd, 1969
———, *Seegeltung in der deutschen Geschichte*, Darmstadt, 1957
Bräckow, Werner, *Die Geschichte des deutschen Marine-Ingenieur-Offizierkorps*, Oldenburg, 1974
Brennecke, H. J., and Kranke, Theodore, *The Battleship Scheer*, London, 1956
Breyer, Siegfried, *Battleships of the World, 1905–1970*, London/New York, 1980
———, *Battleships and Battlecruisers, 1905–1970*, London/New York, 1973
Breyer, Siegfried, and Koop, Gerhard, *Die deutsche Kriegsmarine 1935–1945*, vols 4 and 5, Friedberg, 1988 and 1989
———, *Von der Emden zur Tirpitz,* 2nd edn, Bonn, 1991
Chesneau, Roger, (ed.), *Conway's All the World's Fighting Ships 1922–1946*, London, 1980
Churchill, Winston S., *The Second World War,* 6 vols, London/Boston, 1948–53
Diwald, Helmut, *Der Kampf um die Weltmeere*, Munich/Zürich, 1980
Dönitz, Karl, *Memoirs: Ten Years and Twenty Days*, with a new Introduction by Jürgen Rohwer, London/Annapolis, 1990
Dülffer, Jost, *Weimar, Hitler und die Marine*, Düsseldorf, 1972
Ewers, Heinrich, *Kriegsschiffbau*, Berlin, 1943
Giessler, Helmuth, *Der Marine-Nachrichten-und-Ortungsdienst*, Munich, 1971
Gladisch, Walter, and Schulze-Hinrichs, Alfred, *Seemannschaft*, Berlin, 1940
Gröner, Erich, *German Warships, 1815–1945*, London/Annapolis, 1991
Güth, Rolf, *Die Marine des deutschen Reiches 1919–1939*, Frankfurt, 1972
Hadeler, Wilhelm, *Kriegsschiffbau*, Darmstadt, 1968
Handbuch zur deutschen Militärgeschichte 1648–1939, edited by Militärgeschichtlichen Forschungsamt, vol. 4/section VIII, Deutsche Marinegeschichte der Neuzeit, Munich, 1979
Herwig, Holger H., *Das Elitekorps des Kaisers*, Hamburg, 1977
Hildebrand, Hans H.; Rohr, Albert; and Steinmetz, Hans-Otto, *Die deutschen Kriegsschiffe, Biographien*, vols 1, 2 and 4, Herford, 1979–81
Hildebrand, Hans H., and Henriot, Ernest, *Deutschlands Admirale 1849–1945,* Vols 1–3, Osnabrück, 1988–90
Hubatsch, Walther, *Die erste deutsche Flotte*, Herford, 1981
———, *Die Kaiserliche Marine*, Munich, 1975
———, (ed.), *Hitlers Weisungen für die Kriegsführung 1939–1945*, 2nd edn, Koblenz, 1983
———, *'Weserübung': Die deutsche Besetzung von Dänemark und Norwegen 1940*, 2nd edn, Göttingen, 1960
Hümmelchen, Gerhard, *Die deutschen Seeflieger 1935–1945*, Munich, 1976
Jung, Dieter; Abendroth, Arno; and Kelling, Norbert, *Anstriche und Tarnanstriche der Kriegsmarine*, Munich, 1977
Koop, Gerhard; Galle, Kurt; and Klein, Fritz: *Von der Kaiserlichen Werft zum Marinearsenal: Wilhelmshaven als Zentrum der Marinetechnik seit 1870*, Munich, 1982
Koop, Gerhard, and Mulitze, Erich, *Die Marine in Wilhelmshaven*, Koblenz, 1987
Lochner, R. K., *Als das Eis brach*, Munich, 1983
Lohmann, Walter, and Hildebrand, Hans H., *Die deutsche Kriegsmarine 1939–1945, Gliederung, Organisation, Stellenbesetzung*, 3 vols, Bad Nauheim, 1956–64
Pemsel, Helmut, *Biographisches Lexikon zur Seekriegsgeschichte*, Koblenz, 1985
Potter, Elmer B.; Nimitz, Chester W.; and Rohwer, Jürgen, *Sea Power: A Naval History*, Annapolis, 1981
Prager, Hans Georg, *Panzerschiff Deutschland/Schwerer Kreuzer Lützow*, Herford, 1981
Raeder, Erich, *My Life*, Annapolis, 1960
Rahn, Werner, *Reichsmarine und Landesverteidigung 1919–1928*, Munich, 1976

Rasenack, F. W., *Panzerschiff Admiral Graf Spee*, Herford, 1977
Rohwer, Jürgen and Hümmelchen, Gerhard, *Chronology of the War at Sea*, London/Annapolis, 1992
Ruge, Friedrich, *Sea Warfare 1939–1945: A German Viewpoint*, London/Annapolis, 1957
Salewski, Michael, *Die deutsche Seekriegsleitung 1935–1945*, 3 vols, Frankfurt/Munich, 1970–75
Sandhofer, Gert, *Das Panzerschiff A und die Vorentwürfe 1920–1928*, Freiburg, 1968
Schmalenbach, Paul, *Die Geschichte der deutschen Schiffsartillerie*, Herford, 1968
Strohbusch, Erwin, *Kriegsschiffbau seit 1848*, Bremerhaven, 1977
Wagner, Gerhard, (ed.), *Lagevorträge des Oberbefehlshabers der Kriegsmarine vor Hitler 1939–1945*, Munich, 1972
Whitley, M. J., *German Capital Ships of World War II*, London, 1989
Zienert, Josef, *Unsere Marineuniform*, Hamburg, 1970

PERIODICALS

Atlantische Welt
Flotte
Jahrbuch der Schiffbautechnischen Gesellschaft
Leinen los
Marine
Marineforum
Marine-Rundschau
Militärgeschichtliche Mitteilungen
Nauticus
Schiff und Zeit
Schiffbau
Schifffahrt International/Seekiste
Tages- und Wochenzeitungen und- Zeitschriften
Truppenpraxis
US Naval Institute Proceedings
Warship
Warship International
Warship Profile
Werft, Reederei, Hafen
Weyer

OTHER SOURCES AND UNPUBLISHED PAPERS

Author's archive
Burkhardt, Hermann (Marine-Oberbaudirektor a.D.), 'Die Entwicklung des Schiffbaumaterials der Deutschen Kriegsmarine'
———, 'Die Entwicklung des Unterwasserschutzes in der Deutschen Kriegsmarine'
———, 'Der Einfluss der Kriegsschiffbaues auf die Entwicklung der Technik'
Cordes, Ludwig (Ministerialdirigent a.D.), 'Diverser Schriftverkehr'
———, 'Principles of Design of Naval Gunmountings used in German Practice', written for the 'Historical Division', 1948/50
Fuchs, Werner (Kadm a.D.), 'Der deutsche Kriegsschiffbau' (1959)
MAN-Archiv, 'Betriebsunterlagen und Beschreibungen der Motorenanlagen der Panzerschiffe *Deutschland, Admiral Scheer, Admiral Graf Spee*'
MAN-Archiv, 'Diverses Schriftgut zur Motorenentwicklung und Geschichte des Schiffsdieselmotors mit Protokollen u.a.m.'
OKM, 'Unterlagen und Richtlinien zur Bestimmung der Hauptkampfentfernungen und der Geschosswahl, 1940'
Pfitzmann, 'Schiffsansprengungen und Kriegserfahrungen'
Dipl.-Ing. Többicke (Marine-Oberbaurat z. Wv.), 'Die Panzerung der deutschen Kriegsschiffe'

BUNDESARCHIV/MILITÄRARCHIV

Schiffbuch-/Kriegstagebuchauszüge: Panzerschiff *Deutschland*/Schwerer Kreuzer *Lützow*; Panzerschiff *Admiral Scheer*; Panzerschiff *Admiral Graf Spee*; Konstruktionspläne: *Deutschland/Lützow, Admiral Scheer, Admiral Graf Spee*
AVKS: Erprobungsprotokolle Panzerschiff *Admiral Graf Spee*
Erprobungsprotokolle Schwingungsmessungen Panzerschiffe
Marinekabinett/Reichsmarineamt/OKM: Ranglisten der Kaiserlichen, Reichs- und Kriegsmarine

Index of Ships